# Table of Contents

# Introduction

This is not a get rich quick book. I wish it was, as I could probably charge at least $1,000 a copy, but then the only person who would get rich would be me, and that isn't the purpose of this book. It is though, a become wealthy slowly kind of book with no guarantees, no short cuts and no fast track to riches. Sorry, but it is not that. But don't give up on this book, as it is full of life changing material. Just not at rocket speed.

This book is for:

- You, if you are just starting out and perhaps taking your first job, and have no idea about what superannuation is, let alone why you should care.

- You, if all of a sudden you have your own income and are just busting to spend it!

- You, as a young adult and suddenly responsible, or maybe married and need to get some semblance of a plan happening.

- You, if – for whatever life's reasons might be – find yourself now in control of your own finances and are not sure where to start, or who to trust. You are "suddenly responsible", and quite understandably, need a helping hand.

- You, if you feel like a fun read.

**So why me?**

I was inspired by my father about the share market. The whole idea of it fascinated me, although I had no idea about what it really was or even meant. It was just this "thing" he spoke about in an animated way, and especially when the shares were going up! I recall Bounty

Oil was a big favourite of his. In reality, I doubt that he knew any more than I did, but he had a passion for it which infused into me. He was a dentist, which frankly did not excite me at all, and although he made some money from the market, I have no idea how much. It was the excitement that spoke to me. He didn't seem to be an investor; more of a speculator. Later on, in life, he definitely became an investor, but my inspiration came from the speculative side. It was exciting, and seemed a great way to make (or lose) a lot of money!

I purchased my first shares on the same basis (clueless), before I was 18, and have been trading and investing continually since then. (Sometimes just as clueless, but more often than not quite well.

I am a specialist accountant and have worked with numbers most of my life. I even had a stint as a Financial Planner and for a time was the Assistant Listing Manager at the Australian Stock Exchange in Perth. For a while, I had an unrestricted Dealer's Licence in Securities, but I am now involved in managing my modest family investments, and most recently included Mortgage Broking as part of my service offering.

I have made lots of financial mistakes, but have had many more successes than disasters, thankfully, and now seeing my kids leave school and grow up realised that none of what I now know is taught at school. I realise by talking to lots of different people, that I actually know quite a bit. I am no expert and I am not fabulously wealthy, but I have managed to build some wealth. I have done lots of different things in my life and plan to do many more. You will learn that I have strong opinions that will help you to avoid some mistakes, and also steer you towards the right path to a slow accumulation of wealth.

I have worked in a wide range of industries and also advised people from all sorts of backgrounds. I say this not to blow my trumpet, but just to let you know that I do have a lot of diverse experience, and am somewhat qualified to offer my opinions. But then you will form your own opinion about that! Offered they will be. What you do with them, I can't control!

The driving force behind this book, is to provide you with some basic assistance, cut through the jargon, and provide suggestions as to a sound basis for building wealth, slowly.

## The Fine Print

Now, I don't know you; your circumstances or your appetite for risk (that is, whether you are a risk taker or not). Because of that, and more particularly because I am not a licensed adviser in securities, nothing I say should be considered as financial advice. You should seek advice that is relevant to you and your circumstances from a properly licensed adviser. I might be able to advise you with regard to obtaining a loan, but only after becoming very familiar with your circumstances, i.e., not as a result of you reading this book.

While I do mention some organisations in this book, all of the opinions are my own. If I speak well of an organisation, it is not because I receive any remuneration from them as a result of my comments or recommendations made in this book. Should you become a client of mine, I would receive commissions in the normal course of business, the details of which would be fully disclosed to you. After all, I have a family to feed as well, and as already said to you, this book is not going to make me rich either!

None of the businesses I mention, neither endorse this book, nor offer any opinion or responsibility in the event you decide to do something as a or result of reading this book and acting on my opinions. At the risk of being very dull, this is general commentary only and does not consider your particular circumstances, needs or objectives. Nor does it take into account the financial needs of any specific person. You should consider your own personal financial situation and needs or seek financial advice before making any decisions based on this information.

Now I would like to introduce you to the 12 Money Beans Rules. What is a money bean for starters? It is that seed, which, if you had some, you could plant and grow wealthy. Well, I have none, but what I can pass on to you is some seeds of knowledge that will let you do it yourself.

**Money Beans 12 Rules**

1. Saving leads to wealth. Savings with compounding leads to much more wealth.

2. Seek independent advice, always.

3. If you don't educate yourself, even just a little, you are limiting your opportunities.

4. If it seems to be too good to be true, it is.

5. Stock tips are well named in that they are generally rubbish and belong in the tip.

6. The market is cruel and doesn't care about you.

7. The market works on fear and greed.

8. Advisers that are tied to a sole provider like a bank are not offering advice; they are providing products which may not be the best products for you.

9. The "safest" products give the least returns.

10. Saving is the path to wealth possibility.

11. Investing well is the path to wealth probability

12. Protecting your wealth is the key to, well protecting your wealth! (Not the deepest rule but just as true as the other 12).

13. Be careful who you trust.[1]

---

[1] So, this guy cannot even count. I understand if you think you have been conned, but stay with it.

## Disclosure

What? More disclosures? Get on with it for crying out loud!

I have a sense of humour (some may disagree, but then they are unlikely to even read this book, so they won't know any different), but, if you **are** seeking serious, check out Dostoevsky in the library. Life can be serious enough without another book rattling on about finance. This is not a finance treatise either. It is simply a guide to make the most of what you have, or will have, or even could have. It is deliberately meant to be an easy read, and for goodness sake, not all at once! Get some Netflix in between, or at least a cappuccino!

## How to use the book

You'd think you would just have to read it, but apparently there is even a guide on how to do that! The way in which the book, was designed was to follow different stages that will present themselves to you as life goes on and my opinions on each of them. There is though no need to read the book in order, but you could. This means if you have an issue to do with a different stage in your life, jump ahead. But then I decided to group it into events in life, like getting a job, getting a loan and investing. This makes more sense since, if later in life, you become suddenly responsible, the same areas might well apply to you, so carry on.

I know life can get busy, which is okay, so for some of you who want to get to the point quickly this is perhaps the best way to use the book. You could copy the Money Beans Rules into Canva or something clever and print them out Every time you need to make a financial decision keep them handy. If I get some time when I create a website, I may make these downloadable, but if not, you can easily do this. If you send me an email, I can make sure you are the first to know when it is live!

If you get stuck, send me an email. If I am not lazing about somewhere, I might even answer it. office@money-beans.com.

You're welcome.

# Money Beans 12 Rules

1. Saving leads to wealth. Savings with compounding leads to much more wealth.

2. Seek independent advice, always.

3. If you don't educate yourself, even just a little, you are limiting your opportunities.

4. If it seems to be too good to be true, it is.

5. Stock tips are well named in that they are generally rubbish and belong in the tip.

6. The market is cruel and doesn't care about you.

7. The market works on fear and greed.

8. Advisers that are tied to a sole provider like a bank are not offering advice; they are providing products which may not be the best products for you.

9. The "safest" products give the least returns.

10. Saving is the path to wealth possibility.

11. Investing well is the path to wealth probability

12. Protecting your wealth is the key to, well protecting your wealth! (Not the deepest rule but just as true as the other 12.

13. Be careful who you trust

# First Job (maybe ever, or maybe after a long time)

**You Got A Job.**

This is a really exciting and also a potentially scary time. And so, it begins; all of a sudden you are responsible (good name for a book don't you think?). It just happened and it's time for you to step up. This means, to get involved in planning your life and not just be a cork bobbing on the water waiting for the current to steer you along. How you treat this job can impact your life going forward in so many ways, because you now have so many decisions, choices, and responsibilities. And you thought you were just going to have to turn up and be showered with money!

It is an interesting contradiction when you think about it. You were busting to get money, but now you have less free time and you are expected to work. Not just work, but if you want to get good at what you do, it means you need to learn, suggest things and improve your work environment along the way. You can choose, even in your first job, to simply turn up and get what you get given, or to get involved and start to learn to chart your own course.

You will also have to make many personal decisions along the way. Making the decisions and making plans is the key to a more successful life. With the first job comes the option to start designing your own life rather than simply reacting to what happens.

*"People who never dream, or never set goals, let life go by day by day letting others determine their destiny. Without advancing your dream through the process of setting plans to reach your goal, you are forced to accept what you have today."* Catherine Pulsifer, "Living The Dream."

## Woohoo - You Get Paid!

Here's where the financial fun starts; it's now time to receive your first pay. You will have filled out forms, which is your "welcome to the world of paperwork". Love it or hate it, you have to deal with it. It will start popping up everywhere in your life. It will become important so set up an A-to-Z file and make sure you open that mail, file it away and keep it handy. Sometimes you can empty your file and keep all your papers in an envelope stored by tax year, reusing your file for the current year. Not too taxing (pun) but keeps everything together so you can find it again. If you are technologically adept, perhaps scan all your paperwork and store in directories that are easily identifiable. Keep the paperwork until you have your e-filing system under control. Maybe setup some cloud storage like Google Drive for when the inevitable happens?

## Time to open a Bank Account

To receive your pay, you will need to open up a bank account. No pressure, but how you manage this might well set your destiny for the rest of your life. Bit dramatic? Maybe, but it's time to get savvy and develop good habits!

Opening an account is not a difficult process. You just have to prove you are who you say you are. In many cases you can do it online and just need some identification, such as:

- a valid Australian driver's licence;

- an Australian passport that has not been expired for more than two years;

- a valid Medicare card with more than two months left to expiry.

Depending on your bank, the verification of these documents can also be done online. Otherwise, you will have to find a bank branch and talk to a real live person. Yes, it's a bit antiquated but it's equally as exciting. After all, think of those fortnightly payments you'll be getting!

Most bank account numbers in Australia consist of two parts. The first of these is the BSB or Bank-State-Branch number. A BSB is a six-digit number that identifies banks and branches across Australia. Its history likely lies in the issuing of cheques that had to pass through a sorting house and for banks to know their origin and who to seek payment from when the cheques were presented. The concept of branch hardly seems to matter, in this Internet fuelled age, but it's still important that you make sure to get it right. What follows the BSB is your account number. That is unique to you.

**Debit Cards and Credit Cards too!**

***Be cautious with Credit cards.***

With your bank account, you can also apply for debit cards which lets you access your own money. This is by far the safest form of card as you cannot spend what you don't have. Simple. Debit cards only allow you to access the exact amount of money you have at any point in time in the bank account linked with your debit card. The card simply provides access to money machines (ATMs, holes in the wall, or automatic teller machines) or to the electronic payments system popular for online shopping, often via a VISA branding. Convenient and safe!

The bank may offer you a credit card. Unlike the debit cards which only give you access to the funds in your bank account at present, these devils (the cards, not necessarily the banks) let you access money you don't have. Credit cards have the potential to be great resources in certain circumstances, but should be avoided if you are a compulsive spender. Yes, I know "those new shoes are so nice........."

Credit cards can attract rewards points, generally at a really poor rate but equally come with annual fees. As long as you pay the whole amount of what you spend monthly then they are fine to use. However, if you don't, you can expect to pay hefty interest; currently upwards of 18%! They also often come with some enticing offers like interest free periods. What that means is if you pay on time and within that period, often 55 days, then NO interest will be charged. Step outside that safe zone and you will be skinned alive with interest charges. So, to put it simply, don't.The other supposedly enticing offer is loyalty points. That is where you spend a huge amount of money to earn points of some to little value depending on which provider is trying to sign you up. Some of the sign on offers can be worthwhile. But at the risk of being boring, you don't really need a credit card until you prove to yourself you can handle it. When I say "handle it", I mean that even if you have this piece of plastic burning a hole in your pocket you can still live within your means. And, so the lessons start!

I use a credit card relentlessly, but equally as relentlessly it is paid on time, I bank the few points, and happy days. But what else would you expect from a cynical accountant?

Interestingly, according to Finder, in the 18-35 age group:

- 39.48% had one credit card

- 17.59% had two credit cards

- 8.36% had three or more credits cards

Just be careful. **Get in the habit of only buying what you can afford and you will be fine.** If you are forever buying on credit, then you must make changes to your lifestyle and learn to say **no**. If you don't, then this will become your norm and its simply not a good plan, unless you want to work for the banks or credit card providers, but without any pay. Say no, "I don't need it to be happy", visit op shops and enjoy what you have.

## Money Beans Rule 10

*Saving is the path to wealth possibility.*

**If you want to live a comfortable life – learn the Habit of Saving.**

The awesome thing, and the issue, here, is that with this sudden influx of earnings comes possibilities. Fun stuff; cars, holidays, parties! All of a sudden there is no more waiting on the Bank of Mum and Dad for handouts. (Well, hopefully not, for their sakes.) But while the short-term rewards are fun and seem important, so is putting some cash aside for a rainy day. You need to be a little squirrel-like. Whilst it might seem boring and dull for now, you certainly won't think so when you can stop working early, or at least feel confident that your lifestyle can be as you want it to be when you want it to be so.

I don't know about you, but I always found the idea of growing old and having to worry each time a bill came through to be 100% something to be avoided. I want to enter my retirement comfortable in the thought that if I decide suddenly to take off for a month somewhere, that I could. That to me is real wealth, **the power of having choices**. Yes, I get it, that at 16 or 18, whenever your first job may come about, that seems kind of old fashioned, and too far away, but you have the power of compounding on your side and need do little else.

I will say that **again** because you only get one chance to use the huge amount of time you have, when you are young to when you retire, to have and enjoy some serious money *doing very little*. It is hard to find a more appealing option than that!

# Power of Compounding

*Save, reinvest the interest, and add more!*

What magic is this? This, according to Albert Einstein is "the most powerful force in the Universe"!

That is a fantastic ally to have, and the sooner you start to have that force with you, that more chance you will have of growing wealth by doing nothing much. Sound good?

It is the basic concept of reinvesting your interest. What? **Warning some maths ahead.**

OK, suppose you had $1000 and could earn 5% interest. That means at the end of one year (interest rates are usually quoted yearly to make them sound bigger), or if we go a little Latin, per annum.

So, after one year you have earned $50 in interest. You can then reinvest the $1000, or if you are smart, and we are working on that, you will invest $1050 and so on.

| End of Year | Invested | Interest paid | Reinvest with interest |
|---|---|---|---|
| 1 | 1,000 | 50 | 1,050 |
| 2 | 1,050 | 53 | 1,103 |
| 3 | 1,103 | 55 | 1,158 |
| 4 | 1,158 | 58 | 1,216 |

| | | | |
|---|---|---|---|
| 5 | 1,216 | 61 | 1,277 |
| 6 | 1,277 | 64 | 1,341 |
| 7 | 1,341 | 67 | 1,408 |
| 8 | 1,408 | 70 | 1,478 |
| 9 | 1,478 | 74 | 1,552 |
| 10 | 1,552 | 78 | 1,630 |

Put simply, you could spend the interest and after 10 years still have your $1000, or reinvest it and have $1630. The following graphs are courtesy of the Moneysmart website, an initiative of the Australian Government.

*$1000 compounded at 5% for 10 years – no additional investment*

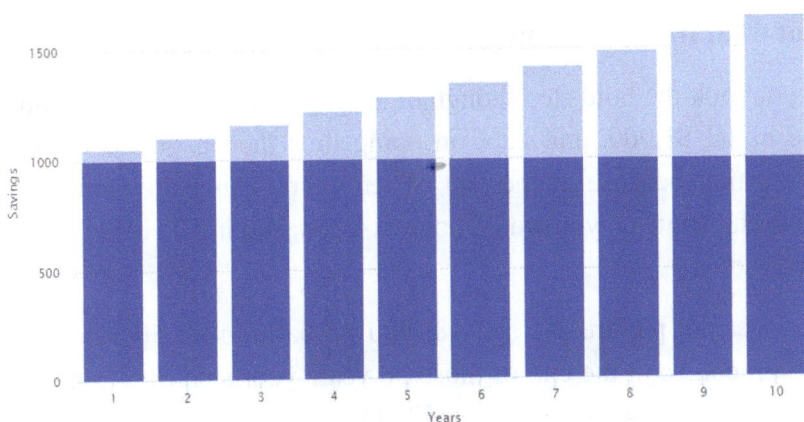

Results

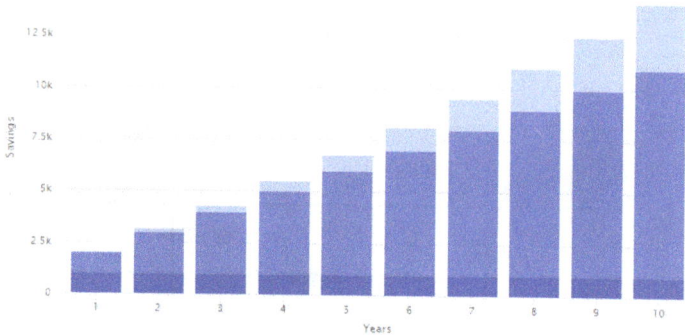

*$1,000 compounded at 5% for 10 years – $1,000 additional investment each year.*

If graphs confuse you, check the scale on the left-hand side. The savings axis in the first graph only goes up to $1,500 but on the second one to $12,500. That means to save more, and let it grow (compounding) you end up with a larger number. Not that surprising, but watching it grow by doing nothing except adding to it is ***magical***.

**But what if you want more?**

If you took the bold step though of adding $1,000 per year on top of the initial $1,000, and kept on doing this; then it gets even more interesting because at the end of ten years, using this simple but powerful strategy, you would have $14,208; and in 30 years $70,673. Not bad!

You get the picture. At age 18, you probably have 50 years until retirement, so at the end of those 50 years your small investment of $1,000 a year would grow to $220,820 ignoring taxes. (Wish we could sometimes.)

Here, though, is where it gets really interesting, as nerdy as that may seem.

Given time is on your side at 18, what if you took your $1000 but then added $5,000 per year (which is $100 per week roughly)? **You would have over $2m at the end of 50 years!**

## Money Beans Rule 1

*Saving leads to wealth. Savings with compounding leads to much more wealth.*

**So, what to do with your pay-packet?**

Depending on your circumstances – whether you're still at home, renting, paying board or not – you ought to be able to set aside some of what you earn to a savings account, or send it off to a couple of accounts. One for investing and the other for a rainy day. What is left, is for you to do what you want. Remember that before this job you didn't earn anything, so use it wisely! When I was a financial planner, I used to ask my clients, "would you survive if you earned 10% less?" Usually they said yes, so I said "okay, why not live like that? Take 10% of what you earn and save it like crazy."

Ideally, then when you get paid your pay will be deposited directly into some sort of bank transaction account. When you are choosing, look for an account with no fees; perhaps set up some sort of linked savings account and one investment account. Often banks will provide higher interest rates (remember our friend, when we are earning it, **is** interest) for regular contributions. Linked accounts make for easier online transferring between your accounts.

One website I use frequently is Canstar. They make comparisons of many bank accounts easier and to the best of my knowledge are independent. This will make choosing easier.

## Money Beans Rule 2

*Seek independent advice; always.*

When choosing your accounts, I wouldn't get too clever, and open too many accounts, because once you start paying tax you, or someone will have to comb through all of these different accounts for details of interest you may have earned or for other transactions as your investment strategy grows. Maybe one transaction, one everyday savings, and one not to be touched. After all, if you have the discipline to do that, you ought to have the discipline to maintain their purpose, and having 10 different accounts won't stop you ransacking your own accounts if you so choose.

Simple? Just do it and set up regular transfers. By this I mean from your transaction account (where the pay goes in, and your spending comes out, a transfer will be to move say $200 to your rainy-day account. It could be a regular transfer setup with the transaction account or manual which means you have to do it each pay period. Automatic means it will just happen; one less job for you.

If you think of your "**don't touch**" savings account as money you do not have access to, unless in an emergency, then you are well on the way to building great savings habits. You will then be able to smile smugly as your friends who don't do this, and most will not, always seem to struggle for an extra bit of money (but not too smugly; it's not that cool to gloat.)

### Summary

1. Compounding is your friend. Use it to grow wealth slowly and for a long time.

2. Setup a transaction account, a savings account and what will become an investment account.

3. As at the date of writing this book (early 2021), interest rates are very low. This may not always be the case, so whilst this may not have too much appeal right now, when rates rise, you will benefit. You are welcome in advance. ☺

# Superannuation

## *Superannuation (Super) is super![2]*

Understand what it is and make good choices. If you want to know what choices, then you will have to read at least the super summary that follows.

This is another old person thing. Right? Who cares about super? Well, you should if you want to be wealthy. "Oh, but that's for retirement and it is so far away." True, but it has built in, the power of compounding, plus more"; "wait, what, better than Einstein?"

What it is simply put, is a deal between you, your employer, the government, and the entity[3] that holds the money – that is your super fund, which is not actually you. Super funds are businesses that receive the money usually from your employer, and then invests it on your behalf. They receive contributions from many different people and are able to pool the money together to then do the investing for you, allocating your share to your personal account based on your contributions. While superannuation is a great asset, super funds do charge fees, and some more than others. (See down a bit for point 1 in the summary that follows.).

Awesome, first job and you are doing deals already. Proud of you! What it is, is more complex than this really, but is a system of rules and structures designed to encourage you to save for your own retirement. There's that word, again! Well guess what, as medical development improves, we are living longer so if you want your retirement to be uber cool, listen up! Also, remember retirement does

---

[2]Warning, Dad Joke.

[3]An entity in this sense might be a company or a trust.

not need to mean work until you drop. If you are smart, and with this book you can be, then retirement could be when you want it to be. No more working, 9 to 5.

The rules make it compulsory for your employer to make a contribution on your behalf to a super fund of your choice. It is part of your wages but designed so that you have something to enjoy when you finally stop work!

Generally, if you receive $450 or more before tax in a calendar month, you should expect to receive super on top of your wages. The minimum you will receive is called the super guarantee, which is currently 9.5% of an employee's ordinary time earnings. This is planned to grow to be 12% by 2027.

Have a look at Moneysmart (again) – "Choosing a super fund, how to compare and choose super funds", not a long read and be informed!

## Money Beans Rule 3

*If you don't educate yourself, even just a little, you are limiting your opportunities*

There is really little point in me regurgitating what is freely available in lots of other places. You wouldn't read it anyway. 😊 But although you may not read any wider, do at least read the next section please. It can make a lot of difference to how much your super fund can grow to. I have deliberately tried to make these bits of information easily digestible, i.e., short.

### Money Beans Super Summary

Well, it is a superannuation summary, but more of a super superannuation summary. (Warning another Dad joke.)

1. Check out the fees that they will want to charge you. These will ferociously consume small contributions, which you will be receiving in your early years particularly. Fees might vary depending on the choice of investments you choose. They ought to be lower for the more risk-free investments like cash, and understandably higher for investments like shares, since there is more work for them to do and they need to maintain their very expensive lifestyles, and flash offices! You could check them out using Superguide, a website dedicated to all thing's superannuation. Since they comply with *Money Beans Rule No 2*, (Independent advice), I am happy to mention them in this book.

2. See if the fund offers insurance and what it costs. This is often deducted for you, but without necessarily asking you, and will also eat away your account balance without any remorse. I cannot give insurance advice, but ask you to question what the benefit might be, and to whom? If you have no dependants, and/or debts, then no insurance could be a better choice.

3. If you're just starting work, you probably can't afford a SMSF yet. A SMSF, while it sounds like a smurf, actually stands for a Self Managed Super Fund which could be more useful when you are earning a higher salary and perhaps have a partner to share it with. Lots of paperwork, lots of responsibility, and even more flexibility is what you get here. In the olden days, i.e. my time, $300k was about the value of assets where it became potentially beneficial to run your own show. This may not be for you at this stage of life necessarily but is something you could consider as your

super fund increases in value. The good news is that you can transfer (rollover) the money in another fund to any other fund including a SMSF.

4. There are also industry funds, often with lower fees and run as not for profits. What that means is that they are run for the benefits of their members, sometimes are industry specific but fairly much open to anyone now. They can have lower fees. Their counterparts are funds offered by the likes of banks and insurance companies called retail super funds. There is though not always a huge diffference but do see point 1 above.

5. As well as the first point about fees, this point can make a **huge** difference to your returns and that is the choice of investment. While you need to seek your own advice, the following is my approach. One basic premise in investing, is that with more risk comes more return. For example, you could choose to have your super with a fund that offers higher risk, often with higher fees, and typically with higher returns. That is when it's up to you to decide if the higher fees might be offset enough by the potential for greater return. With that in mind, many of the funds will offer choices in the type of investments made on your behalf. This leads to the fascinating subject of asset classes.

## 6. Asset Classes

| Asset Class | Risk |
|---|---|
| Cash term deposits, bonds | Low |
| Managed Funds | Low risk<br>Medium risk<br>High risk |
| Shares | Low risk<br>Medium risk<br>High risk |

6. If I was advising, which I am not, someone who is younger should be more inclined to accept some risk. This is because you should likely be looking to a long term to hold the investment, and therefore can manage a little volatility. What this means, is that at age 18 and with 50 working years ahead of you, I question any reason to be conservative. That is how I feel; you may feel differently and that is your choice, but make it with knowledge. Volatility simply means prices will go up and down, but given a longer term generally up. No guarantees, but check out this graph of the ASX200 for the last 9 years. Apart from the Covid-19 incidence, it is heading up. There are fluctuations, of course, but overall, it is heading up. Even with Covid-19, you can see that the market is still looking like it will be picking up shortly (fingers crossed, as we can only guess at this point).

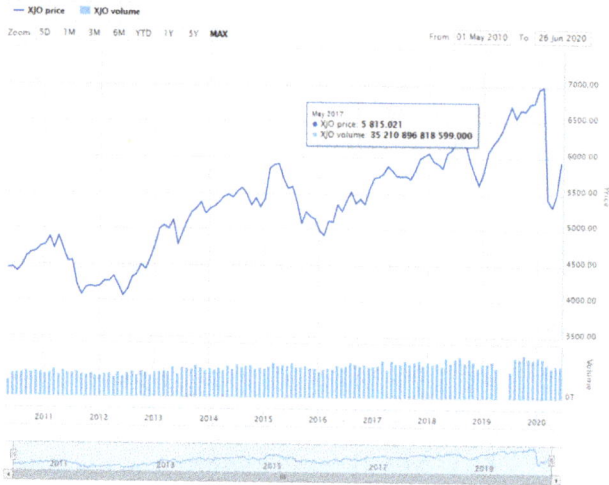

*Graph from asx.com.au*

7. If you were suddenly responsible, at age 60, my thinking would understandably be different, and less risk is more likely better for you. It depends on what other assets are available to you, and whether you want to sleep without a care in the world. Seek independent advice based on your circumstances (Moneybeans Rule 2).

8. You can add additional money to your superannuation pot of gold. Making additional contributions to your super account can make a noticeable difference to your financial future, (recall compounding, Money Bean Rule 1) The earnings paid on earnings can markedly assist growing your balance over time. And you may also be able to lower your taxable income through what is called salary sacrificing. There are, like all things tax, a bunch of rules but this can be a tax effective strategy for a later stage in life.

## Conclusion about Super

So that is all I need to say about super. Many people as they go through life put more and more into superannuation. As long as you save somewhere, it may not make that much difference, except for, and this is a big one – flexibility.

Because of the deal you made with the government, there are rules like you would not believe in the superannuation arena. If you build your wealth outside of super, then you can do what you want with your savings. Not so with super.

Before you say that's not fair, you need to consider that: -

1. There are tax breaks on the money super funds earn. (Translates to the superannuation fund enjoys the benefit of low taxation rates).

2. Your employer contributes as a consequence of the deal (money for nothing, in a sense)

3. The balance of a superannuation fund might be protected from the likes of creditors, if things go bad for you in business.

It comes down to a balance that suits your needs. By the time it is starting to matter, you would be smart to see a financial planner and make a plan. You may notice frequently, done to death quotes about failing to plan, but I quite like this one: -

*"All successful people, men and women are big dreamers. They imagine what their future could be, ideal in every respect, and then they work every day toward their distant vision, that goal or purpose."*
*— Brian Tracy, **Personal Success***

Oh, and what I meant about starting to matter, is when your balance gets higher, and you are in a position to add more than just the amount your employer adds on your behalf. That is the beginnings of choices and strategies around saving for a first home, investing generally and the good stuff. Oh yes, there is lots more!

# Taxation – we all benefit from it but no one likes paying it!

*You will have to pay tax when you earn more than the minimum threshold ($18,200), so keep records and don't be a smarty pants.*

Taxation is a system of raising money from people earning income (taxpayers) to fund all the things that governments do, like providing hospitals, roads, services, and inventing countless rules to govern us by, including the payment of pensions and a whole raft of things that keeps the country running. So, when they say they are spending money, it is your taxes, as well as any money the Government may decide to borrow. The Government has no money of its own, with the exception of money from assets that are sold.

What this means to you is you have to first make yourself known to the Australian Taxation Office and apply for a Tax File Number which will be your unique identifier forever. This is totally free and starts with downloading an on-line form from https://identityservice.auspost.com.au/ato/landing. After this, you will need to arrange for an interview at Australia Post where you will have to provide proof of identity, supported by original documents. Since mine is so old, I am not 100% sure of what it is. However, it will be highly likely to include your original birth certificate, Medicare card, driver's licence or passport, and possibly proof of your address. The great thing is, you only need to do it once.

A tax file number is considered a private thing so don't give it out willy nilly. Oh, that just means just be a little sensible. It is a nine-digit number like 123-456-789. That's it, but that's you, forever!

## Tax Declaration

As you might expect, now that you are working and earning money, you have to pay tax. Your employer will get you to complete and sign a Tax Declaration form which you can find at https://www.ato.gov.au/forms/tfn-declaration/. This tells the ATO that you are working for a particular person or company and includes their details. In fact, once you have completed your details you simply need to give it to the person paying you. Easy.

You will need your:

- employer's Australian business number (ABN)

- employment type (for example, full time, part-time, casual)

- employers' default super fund details

- name

- unique superannuation identifier (USI) of your nominated super fund and its ABN – don't worry this will be explained to you by your employer. If not, ask. After all you are a grown up now, or close!

That will start the ball rolling and each week or fortnight as you get paid you will receive a payslip showing how much you earned before tax (your gross pay), how much tax was deducted, and occasionally depending on how much you earn, how much was contributed to your nominated superannuation fund.

Question 9 on the Tax Declaration Form can stump some people and it works like this: -

**Question 9 – Do you want to claim the tax-free threshold from this payer?**

The tax-free threshold is the amount of income you can earn each financial year that is not taxed. By claiming the threshold, you reduce the amount of tax that is withheld from your pay during the year.

Answer "yes" if you want to claim the tax-free threshold, you are an Australian resident for tax purposes, and one of the following applies:

- you are not currently claiming the tax-free threshold from another employer; or

- you are currently claiming the tax-free threshold from another payer and your total income from all sources will be less than the tax-free threshold.

Clear as mud. Welcome to the world of tax. If you see the table below, $18,200 is the current tax-free threshold. If you had two jobs and expected to earn more than $18,200 from both then you can only say "yes" on the form to **one** of the employers. However, it all gets sorted out in the wash when you lodge your tax return.

**Tax Rates**

Below are the tax rates for the financial year ended 30 June 2021. In Australia, the financial year is from 1st July to 30th June of the following year. I have no idea why the calendar year is not used, but then again why were there ever 12 inches in a foot? It makes sense to be 10 as that is how many toes I have. (hidden Dad joke)

**Australian income tax rates for 2020/21 (residents)**

| Income thresholds | Rate | Tax payable on this income |
|---|---|---|
| $0 – $18,200 | 0% | Nil |
| $18,201 – $45,000 | 19% | 19c for each $1 over $18,200 |
| $37,001 – $120,000 | 32.5% | $5,092 plus 32.5% of amounts over $45,000 |
| $120,001 – $180,000 | 37% | $29,467 plus 37% of amounts over $120,000 |
| $180,001 and over | 45% | $51,667 plus 45% of amounts over $180,000 |

So, let's say you earn $34,000 per year, your tax will be calculated as follows: -

$34,000 - $18,200 which is $15,800 and then multiply this by 19c to arrive at $3,002.

You can earn up to $18,200 tax free!

At the top end of this, are the high-income earners. No one likes to pay 45% of what they earn and many take steps, often legal, to minimise it. Bottom line advice, yes generally it is OK as long as you make good investment decisions., Don't be driven by, "oh but its tax deductible". It may not give the best result. But then if you are starting out, this is not an issue for you, yet. By the time you get to this sort of income you can and should choose someone to guide you.

*Money Beans Rule 11*

Investing well is the path to wealth probability.

## Tax Returns

I mentioned earlier that the amount of tax you need to pay in total from all sources of income gets considered against the tax that you have paid, or has been paid on your behalf every year at tax time. Simply put all of your income gets added together, including any interest you earn on your savings, any dividends or trust distributions you receive less any deductions you might have to arrive at your taxable income. Paid on your behalf just means that the employer has taken it from your pay, and paid it to the tax office. That is why the system is called PAYG or pay as you go. It is not that the government doesn't trust you, (after all they hardly know you), but it's much easier for all and beats getting a large bill in a year's time!

The tax payable is calculated on this total figure and that is what you owe, less what you have paid and any imputation credits. See dividends later on in this book. For the most part, when you start off, you will not have too many deductions. Deductions are simply expenses that you must incur to do your job. Unfortunately, the cost of getting to and from work is not tax deductible, but cleaning a uniform you are required to wear might be. The ATO provides some useful information on this, "Deductions you can claim".

You can lodge your return online, but don't forget any of these loans you may have had in the past:

- Higher Education Loan Program (HELP)
- VET Student Loan (VSL)
- Student Financial Supplement Scheme (SFSS)

- Student Start-up Loan (SSL)

- ABSTUDY Student Start-up Loan (ABSTUDY SSL)

- Trade Support Loan (TSL)

The Australian Taxation Office provides a handy calculator here. https://www.ato.gov.au/Calculators-and-tools/Host/?anchor=STLoanRepay#STLoanRepay/questions

**How to lodge a tax return**

If your affairs are simple and you are OK with filling in a few items you can do it yourself:

To lodge online with myTax, follow these steps:

- Create a myGov account

- Link your myGov account to the ATO.

- Lodge with myTax

Otherwise, you might use a tax agent and pay them a small fee. Often this is the best course of action. If they are doing a good job, they will get you organised and you can rest easy knowing it is all correct.

If you are preparing and lodging your own tax return, you have from 1 July to 31 October each year to lodge it. If you lodge online in August or September, most of your information will already be pre-filled in your tax return. You'll be less likely to leave something out. The ATO already knows what interest and dividends you have earned so don't be a smarty pants, and just do it properly.

If you receive share dividends, you will receive statements; same for managed funds; and your bank account in July will generally show what interest you may have earned during the year, so you will need to keep track of this. A simple A to Z folder from somewhere like Officeworks will be fine. Often the managed funds take a while to report since they have lots of numbers to add up. (sarcasm alert)

## Down the track – as Your Career Grows. Where to Invest.

It makes little difference if you aspire to be a CEO or run your own plumbing business, each requires hard work and as you progress towards achieving those goals, you will, or should earn as you more, and therefore have more opportunities to save more. Not saying, for a moment that you need to save it all, but do you really need a brand-new car, when a late model, low mileage model might save you thousands of dollars? "Oh great", I can hear you moan, another parent!

But rewards, and high-powered toys aside, you will also be tempted by holidays and new clothes. (Yes, I know you will). If you though maintain a healthy finance balance in your life, you should always have a surplus of income. If not, then there should be good reason why not, else you are out of sync and that is unsustainable. Sorry, but someone has to tell you. It is called living beyond your means and leads to continued and severe unhappiness.

Budgeting is out of the scope of this book, but is just a high-powered word or concept that means you need to live within your means. If you spend more than you earn, stop it. Do without something until you can afford it and be really careful of debt. It is so easy to take, and not so easy to repay. All this means is that it should be taken on board to reach clear goals that I agree with! Things like sensible cars, first homes, investment properties and investing might be all good reasons to take on debt, but then you knew I would l say that!

Smaller amounts for holidays are OK. I understand the temptations, but often people borrow to live a lifestyle they simply cannot manage. If you want two jobs, one your day job and the other to repay your debts, that might be ok. Personally, I would rather wait, and spend my day reading a book or cooking. I can wait another year for a different car.

**OK perhaps a little more on budgeting is appropriate.**

A budget is a financial plan and is all about how you are going to make ends meet. It is about sitting down to understand the costs you can control (fixed costs) and the costs that are variable (increase or decrease with use; think of electricity) and those that are optional like ice-cream or chocolates, (apparently).

What you have to do is make a list everything you spend your money on and convert it all to a monthly amount. So, if you spend say $100 per week on groceries, then that becomes $433 per month. The calculation is, 100*52 / 12.

Then add all of these up, and see which you can vary. Probably few. But there will be some which are optional. Identify these.

Put at the top of the list your take home pay (also converted to monthly). Take home pay means what you get in your pocket. Don't include superannuation since that is for a future you. It is only the net pay.

It might look like this:

| Pay (net)[4] | | 4000 |
|---|---|---|
| Less expenses | | |
| Rent | 1500 | |
| Electricity | 200 | |
| Groceries | 400 | |
| Car | 150 | |
| Total | | <u>2250</u> |
| Shortfall/Surplus | | <u>1750</u> |

[4]Means, after the tax is taken out.

Do this for a while, say 3 months, and then you will know your average costs. But remember some things like perhaps tyres, won't recur for years, so you can estimate a monthly cost for these based on say 3 years. Similarly, for registration.

Then you can use this average figure as your budget figure and start to report against your budget. This might look a little like the table below.

| | Budget | Actual | |
|---|---|---|---|
| **Pay**<br>Less expenses | | | 4000 |
| Rent | 1500 | 1500 | |
| Electricity | 200 | 250 | |
| Groceries | 400 | 600 | |
| Car | 150 | 120 | |
| Total Expenses | 2250 | 2470 | |
| Shortfall/Surplus | | | 1530 |

What it does is help you track where your money went. Some bank accounts actually help you identify this as well by classifying your spending.

There is a healthy surplus in this example, but what if there was not? What if your bank balance was getting lower and lower? Without doing a budget or tracking your spending you would not know why.

If you understand where it goes, you could start to budget saving as an expense. Sound like an oxymoron[5] It probably is. Here are a few

---

[5]The Cambridge Dictionary defines oxymoron as two words used together that have, or seem to have, opposite meanings.

more oxymorons; totally irrelevant but kind of fun – *ill health, found missing, impossible solution, original copy and old news.*

For some more clear tips on budgeting and much more have a good read of "How to do a Budget", to be found at the Moneysmart website. Why do I keep mentioning them ?, see Money Beans Rule 2!

# What to do with all this money? Where to Invest? It's all too confusing.

So, back to the story. Now you may have finished school, perhaps working in a trade or you are at uni. Or, if you are suddenly responsible at a mature age, find yourself in a job where you are full time and earning much more, than ever before. Fantastic!

You have choices. Lots of choices. I am not going to advise you, because that is not the point of this book. I am though, going to share my biases and strong opinions. Actually, I am not allowed to advise you. There are many good financial planners out there, but recall the Money Beans Rule 2. Choose someone independent and perhaps talk to a few. They often give a little time for free and see who resonates. After all you should feel some trust and find someone who answers your questions without speaking down to you.

Ultimately though you will choose, or should choose what feels comfortable for you. If you have a vibe, follow it, but remember since you have time on your side you should most likely take on a little risk. But then you have to also sleep well and not be worried about it, else the stress of it all will cause you to get ill and you never get to enjoy your future nest egg. That is simply pointless.

Your choices with this new found extra income are to: -

A.   Spend it. **Nope!**

B.   Continue doing the split[6] thing. **Yes**

---

[6]Moving money to different accounts and then leaving then the heck alone.

C. Move more to super and more to saving. – **Maybe**

D. Do B but add investing. **Yes.**

## The Shares vs Real Estate Dichotomy

The main point of the above heading was to use a word I have never used before, and most likely will never use again. But I digress, whilst I try to appear clever.

Like many things in life, there are clear divisions as to what the right choice to make is, and there are usually sound arguments in support of both. Unless you are one eyed like I am. What am I talking about?

I am talking about investing in shares in listed companies versus investing in the real estate market. It's a bit like the Holden vs Ford or Mercedes vs BMW arguments; both are good, but you are either on one side or the other. Whatever you choose, remember *Money Beans Rules 2 and 3.*

My fundamental investment strategy is to match your strategy with your stage in life. It gets a little more complicated if you have the need to be suddenly responsible later in life, and like all investment decisions you should seek professional advice.

The strategy that I have followed, and would counsel my kids to follow, follows the stages of life which are typically as follows:

*Investment Planning Cycle*

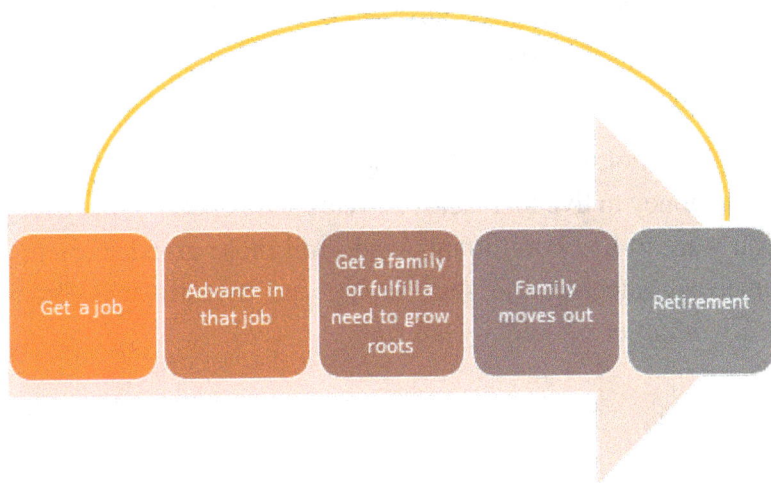

© Money Beans 2021

As this lovely picture shows, or is meant to show, your income or earning potential should grow until you start to wind down and eventually retire. Your investment income should do the inverse and be there to replace your work income. However, the desire to own our own homes is strong and often clouds the cold-hearted facts of numbers. I understand, and having recently rented, I would much prefer to own my own home, regardless of the opportunity cost[7]!

As you advance in your careers and businesses, you ought to earn more, therefore can save more and eventually the income from what you save should fund your retirement. Add to that your superannuation benefits and suddenly retirement is looking good! According to the Australian Institute of Health and Welfare, compared with their

---

[7]opportunity cost simply means what is the lost opportunity of tying money up in say a house. It is the cost of doing one thing as compared to another. In this example it might be the cost of owning a house as against investing the same amount of money in shares.

counterparts in 1881–1890, boys and girls born in 2015–2017 can expect to live around 33 and 34 years longer, respectively. In Australia, a boy born in 2015–2017 can expect to live to the age of 80.5 years and a girl would be expected to live to 84.6 years compared to 47.2 and 50.8 years, respectively, in 1881–1890.

So, like it or not, if you want to stop work at age 60 you better have enough money to live for at least 20 years and hopefully much longer. If you want to live comfortably, and spoil those grandchildren, and yourselves, listen up and start saving and investing wisely. "Oh but, I will never get old", yeah right.

# The Money Beans Golden Investment Plan

To match the earning/investment cycle, here is the Money Beans Golden Investment Plan. This is general advice only and may not be a great plan for you but this is what I did and it has mostly worked for me.

**Buy your own home**

Invest in shares, and save cash until you make enough money to put a deposit on your home. You need a sizeable deposit to allow for minimal monthly repayments. Importantly, you further need to have repayments that you can afford. Choose your house modestly and stay afloat financially. Wanting to live a Kardashian lifestyle on a low income is a recipe for unhappiness. You can always renovate, later on. Keep it simple and be happy!

Real estate is a merry-go-round. Once you are on the ride, it is fine if houses go up in value. (hard to imagine when it wouldn't be?) That is called a capital gain, and is tax free income! However, there are fine high transaction costs with property, including an evil thing called stamp duty. This is the government's way of saying, "Thank you very much, we will take a chunk of that and give you nothing in return." In years gone by, capital gains were almost guaranteed, and were quite sizeable at that – especially over longer periods. I simply don,t know if that will be the case going forwards, when the average house price is quite high already. According to Landgate, the median sale price for houses in the metropolitan area of Perth was around $500,000 and in Sydney, by comparison was $1.1m in December 2019. Growth from here? I don't know; possibly? probably? who knows?

Regardless, we, as a nation, like to own our own homes. Probably so we can paint every wall a different colour and answer to no one. That is the Australian way and I support it 100%! If you can, not having some real estate agent inspecting your house and marking you down on this and that every few months, is worth a lot!

It's interesting, though, as we might think our levels of home ownership are high, Australia is only ranked 42nd in the world. In fact, we're just ahead of the US, NZ and France, while being way behind Romania, Singapore and Slovakia who came 1st, 2nd and 3rd. Interesting trivia? Possibly.

**Pay it off as soon as you can**

Interest payments on your own home are not tax deductible. This means you are taxed on your income regardless of what you pay towards owning your own home. Conversely, interest on borrowed money to fund investments is tax deductible. So much so, if your investment income is $10,000 and your interest is $1,000, then this $1,000 can be claimed against the tax payable on your income. This is called gearing and is only for the brave and sometimes the foolhardy. You might have guessed it, that was me. But it may not be for you. If you're thinking of negatively gearing your property, you'd definitely need advice on this one! It works well when it works, and is like a bad cold when it does not. It has destroyed many investors' box of gold, so beware. But I digress.

Paying your house off is like winning the lottery. No more repayments; no more rent; no more money going out of your clutches; you get choices.

When you borrow money for a home loan, the term might be 25 to 30 years. It is a big decision and a large commitment.

## OK, the Home is Paid off; Next Step!

This opens up a wide range of choices. A strategy that I quite like is, with appropriate advice, borrow against the house to extend your investment possibilities. This all depends on your income, your partner's income, and a whole host of things that I don't know about you, so again, no advice intended or offered.

Whether it is for another house, a unit, or even shares or perhaps managed funds, that is up to you, and the possibilities are endless. Seek financial planning advice but understand you could choose any of:

1. More real estate;

2. Different real estate; townhouses or units perhaps, maybe even in another city[8]?;

3. Managed Funds/ETFs (pooled investments where a manager makes the investment decisions);

4. Direct Shares – local;

5. Direct Shares – international;

6. Any mix of the above depending on your available resources and risk appetite;

7. Doing nothing, but that is plain dull. (Actually, not an option, delete this!).

Note that I have deliberately excluded cryptocurrencies, options, derivatives, forex, etc; not because I do not understand them, but because I doubt that you truly do. I do understand them a little, but choose to stay away. The closest that I come to these types of securities[9] in my trading is CFDs or Contracts for Difference. The

---

[8] Diversification
[9] Many of these are derivatives which means based on a security but not actually the security. (yawn....)

former might be okay, but in my view, and probably ignorance, are more in the former line of speculation. I have dallied with options trading but it was too time consuming, or maybe I was just not good at it. Covered call options are interesting but not for this book.

As an interesting point, many of these "strategies" are touted as risk free and although they can have spectacular returns, they can equally as well have devastating losses. I am really only discussing investing, and not speculating. There is a massive difference.

## Money Beans Rule 4

*If it seems too good to be true, it is.*

I am big enough to admit that analysing the effects of economic policy on global trends and the likely effects on currency pairs is way beyond what I spend my time thinking of, or in reality truly comprehend! The few make lots of money on these types of investments while the majority fund the few.

Back to the story; the point of which was to pay off your house, then use your surplus funds to wisely invest (not speculate) to grow some real wealth, slowly and with patience. If it is shares that you choose to invest in, you should generally be investing with a minimum 5-year view. Again, that is my opinion in an ideal world. However, things can and do change and circumstances will arise, and its therefore advice which often I don't follow! I realise that makes it hard to take me seriously. It's OK you don't have to; you just have to realise that things change and so should your investing philosophy. It might sound counter intuitive, but sometimes sticking to your guns can cost you big time, so it's important to be flexible as well. Having said that there is always a counter, school of thought which, although frustrating, makes it interesting.

Instead of shares, you could choose real estate, or even a mix of the two. It really depends on your surplus funds and your perceived opportunities. Just try not to overextend your borrowing. Should circumstances change, this can bite, and it hurts. The older you get, the more it hurts as the time to rebuild what you might have lost is not be available to you anymore. Logically, as we advance in years, (yes younger people, time will pick you up and will carry you along as well,) the more conservative we should become. That is incontrovertible, but there are always those who love the risk and it can become a drug. In saying that, with the risk comes some wisdom, and it is not until you learn when to cut your losses that your wisdom grows. There is no need to gain that "wisdom" for most people. What this means is invest wisely, diversify, listen to trusted advisers and use time as your friend.

In particular, don't listen to tips, and remember ***Money Beans Rule No 5***.

---

### Money Beans Rule 5

---

*Stock tips are well named in that they are generally rubbish and belong in the tip.*

**What I like, and don't like about both real estate and shares:**

| | Real Estate | Shares |
|---|---|---|
| **What I do like about both** | Your own home is a castle. "Feel the serenity"<br><br>No snooping real estate agents<br><br>Paint your walls any colour you like, even purple! | Diversity of opportunity, markets and themes as well as ways to invest. |
| **What I don't like about real estate and do like about shares.** | Expensive and can be risky if developing or renovating.<br><br>All in, cannot sell just a window if you need cash! | Liquidity and ability to sell small parcels if required. |

|  | High transaction costs including:<br><br>• Agents fees<br>• Stamp Duty<br>• Conveyancing<br>• Mortgage costs | Low transaction costs including:<br><br>• No Agents fees<br>• Much lower brokerage fees<br>• No Stamp Duty<br>• No conveyancing. |
|---|---|---|
|  | Can need up to 60 days to settle and often the buyer is allowed 21 days to find finance | Settlement in as little as three days.<br><br>Quick settlement and can trade again using funds before settlement if required as payment guaranteed. |
|  | Entry price is high – minimum of say $250k for a unit in southern Woop Woop[10] | Minimum parcel of shares in Australia is generally $500. It is possible to trade on overseas exchanges with much less. |

10 Woop-woop is a fictional place in most states which is more than 2 hours from nowhere in particular. Upper woop-woop is even further away

I have owned numerous houses and made some money on most; not so much lately. The rule with buying a house, in my not so humble view, most; not... is to buy well. Don't get emotional, and wait until you get the price that makes sense. If your offer is knocked back, don't take it personally. After all, the seller wants the best price they can get as much as you want the cheapest price you can get. It is said that a good price is where neither the buyer nor the seller is happy.

There is always another house, and the people who pay too much get emotionally attached. Perhaps another buyer can better afford to pay more, but if it is your first house, you can't. If you are an expert real estate analyst, then paying up may make sense, but if you are not, the same may not apply to you.

Also, don't forget **Money Beans Rules 2 and 3.** Take your time, speak to many real estate agents, educate yourself. This is a major purchase. Although you could consider using a buyer's agent, who is supposed to be an expert on your side, this can be an expensive option, and an honest real estate agent might work just as well. Talk to them, understand the language, detect the hype. When you strike an accord, value it, respect their time and look at their reviews. Why not take along a buddy who can observe more than you can, and get another opinion?

Do your research and become a bit of an expert. How do you know what to pay if you have not done as much as some basic comparisons? Really put in some hours on this; and compare and contrast as many homes as you can. It is for most people the largest purchase they will ever make so get involved, do your homework, and do it again. This is not a time to be lazy.

# So now to the Stock Market – What it is, and why might you want to participate.

*Shares are good. The trick is which ones. Read on.*

I could rabbit on for hours or maybe days; or even perhaps bore you to tears forever in just a few minutes. However, in the interest of everyone's time, I'll do my best to summarise. I know that if this section, or even this book is too long you will most likely never read it. Besides there are far more eloquent authors than me, who do go on and on; and loads of free advice; but chances are you will probably not read that either. So here goes, all you need to know about the stock market in as short a time as possible. (I will try and make it entertaining; you judge). Okay, here goes...

The stock market exists as a place where companies can raise money from investors. That is the primary market and an environment where prospectuses abound full of glossy pictures, wonderful projections and forecasts, and an abundance of reasons why you, potential investor, should invest. It is not much different to the guy selling the multi-food grater at the fair. Promises and stories as to why you should hand over your hard-earned money. In very bullish markets (see glossary), these are printed faster than Mills and Boones books and often with as much promise. Similarly, they can have sad endings when the companies run out of money. Spoiler alert: investors do not always live happily ever after. But I digress.

Companies are separate legal entities. OK, losing you. A legal entity is a structure that exists separately from its members or shareholders or directors. It can do business in its own name, and can own assets.

It is managed by Directors who make decisions on behalf of its shareholders. So, what is a shareholder?

If you think of a company as a pie (and who doesn't like to think of pie?), then a share is a slice of pie. You can carve the pie up into lots of slices, therefore having lots of shareholders. Some companies have billions of shares, some only a few million. A share is an ownership in the company but is not the right to make decisions for the company, although collectively shareholders in theory, could (In reality, though,for the company the majority of shareholders influence decisions, but not so much the retail investors which are most of us.) Larger blocks of shares might be held by institutional investors who can sway decision making, but the Mums and Dads seldom have any impact on decision making.

So back to the prospectus story. Suppose a few mates and I have a company, the Excellent Company, and we each have some shares. We decide we want to float[11] our shares on the stock exchange to raise some more money so we can develop our Excellent product range even more. We need a prospectus to raise this money. This is eventually an approved document that is scrutinised by the Stock Exchange before giving permission to list the shares. Listing simply means that a Stock Exchange has approved the Prospectus and will allow investors to use their exchange to buy and sell shares on what is called a secondary market. The additional shares are made available to trade on the market or in the first instance be offered to investors via the prospectus. These offerings are sometimes referred to as IPO's, or Initial Public Offerings.

---

11 According to Investopedia, Floating stock is the number of shares available for trading of a particular stock. Floating stock is calculated by subtracting closely-held shares and restricted stock from a firm's total outstanding shares. Closely-held shares are those owned by insiders, major shareholders, and employees.

Prior to listing, the Excellent Company will have to convince a broker (authorised person to raise money and provide financial advice) to be their sponsor and offer the shares to their clients and even to other brokers. What this means is that the broker has to convince investors that the deal is a really good one and investors will make money by investing in the Excellent Company. Confused? Perhaps an example will de-confuse you. Perhaps it won't?

Let's say that the Excellent Company has developed technology that does something better, but needs $5m to carry out more research and development. The $5m that they plan to spend, as well as what they disclose about how the technology works will be reviewed by "experts" whose disclaimer[12] will be longer than their report and who might advise that if the technology is successful then the Excellent Company will make mega-bucks. This is the potential that is offered to the new shareholders to benefit in, from the ground floor. Imagine buying into the CSL float at $2.40, which was around the price at which shares were offered to the public in 1984. In the beginning of January, 2021, they were worth $283 each according to the market. Whilst I may sound cynical, there are many duds in new offerings and as a new investor you might be well advised to stick with companies with Directors who have at least some experience in running a business. On the other hand, there are so many industry interrupters that have become successful and who have zero business experience. That is the art of picking new investments. However, yet again I digress.

So, the broker rings his clients, talks with other brokers who ring their clients and so on and so forth until the money is in the bank, also

---

[12] A disclaimer is a long-winded document that says someone has reviewed something and used their expert knowledge to form an opinion but takes no responsibility in the event they are wrong.Closely-held shares are those owned by insiders, major shareholders, and employees.

known as "the issue is fully subscribed". Watch Bad Banks on SBS On Demand to see what happens behind the scenes!

The prospectus which lists loads of exceptionally boring information, also contains an application form that says you can apply for so many shares at a particular issue price per share. It might be 10,000 shares at $0.20 because the company is not only trying to raise money but must have a certain number of shareholders to be able to list its shares. The ASX rules require "that to list, a company must satisfy minimum admission criteria, including structure, size, free float and number of shareholders. Your company must have at least 300 non-affiliated shareholders with holdings valued at a minimum of A$2,000 each, and a free float of at least 20%."

After the company lists on the Stock Exchange its shares can then be traded on a stock market. That is what is called the secondary market where the company is no longer directly involved. This is where we can sell our great new shares to someone else. To keep the business orderly, this secondary market is managed under a set of rules administered by the ASX and sometimes ASIC. Put cynically, these bodies are there to contain the wild and boundless speculations that might be made in their absence. The administrators of those rules play a very important role to keep companies from bending the truth and making outrageous claims, as well as to provide a sense of confidence in the market. They are not there to guarantee anything as to the companies' claims, other than to try and keep them honest.

If the Excellent Company said it was going to make 3 squillion dollars in profits and had no viable basis to that claim, their corporate butts would be kicked and the shares might be suspended from trading, as they should be. Similarly, the way in which accounts are prepared and reported are scrutinised to ensure they comply with Accounting Standards and are not too creative. Creative means embellishing the good, ignoring the bad and confusing the many.

The regulators try to make sure the market is an even playing field. This is a good thing as it provides, or tries to provide, an arena where informed decisions can be taken. That is all anyone can ask for, and why I am not a fan of, say, cryptocurrencies. Yes, I know, you may all argue that you know someone who made a fortune; blah blah blah. However, because I need the last word), I'll point out that for everyone who did, there are hundreds who lost their investment.

All right, I hear you glazing over. Maybe this will help.

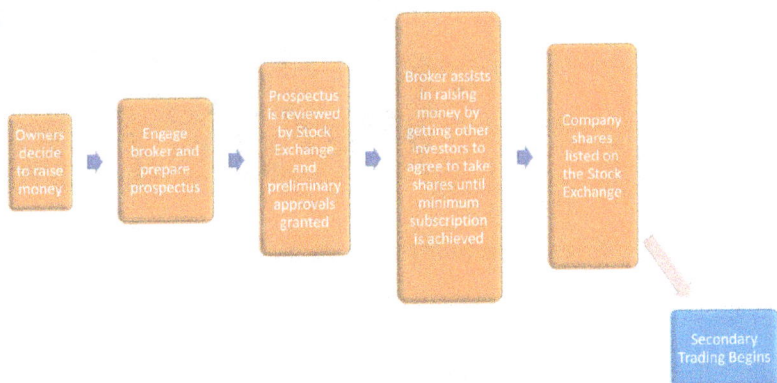

Owners decide to raise money → Engage broker and prepare prospectus → Prospectus is reviewed by Stock Exchange and preliminary approvals granted → Broker assists in raising money by getting other investors to agree to take shares until minimum subscription is achieved → Company shares listed on the Stock Exchange → Secondary Trading Begins

For many investors, they will avoid IPO's and only begin to trade shares in the secondary market where the market has decided the share price compared to Excellent Company's peers and their performance, because, you guessed it, shares will go up and down in value. That is called sometimes volatility but more often the constant fight between bulls and bears. Bulls think everything is good or better and bears are the naysayers and believe in gloom and doom. That is the reason for the bull in Wall St, the home of the US Stock Exchange.

Choosing which shares to buy, when to buy, and when to sell is determined by your goals, your time frame and your appetite for volatility and risk (yet again), and so many other factors that are personal to you, which is why I cannot advise you. I mean, I could, but I am not licensed to and won't. ☺

What you need to understand is that there is speculation, trading, and investing, and they are all different. You will get advice from your hairdresser, the taxi driver and even Uncle Freddie. Most of this is often speculation, and much of it, although well intentioned, is not advice at all. (Remember Money Beans Rule 5). You will find people with bias to all sorts of industries and commodities telling you that this is good and that is good. Whilst occasionally these "tips" might work out, that is likely going to lead to disappointment more often than not. A longer-term strategic approach will lead to more predictable results.

Speculating is holding a view that something will go up in value and buying something based on that view. It could be gold (actual gold), or an exchange Traded Fund that solely specialises in gold, or shares in a gold producing company.

Trading is a shorter-term proposition than investing and is based on a person's view of what is happening in the market, or because of trends observed on Charts. You may have heard of day traders who make trades based on their views and close out (for profit or loss) their positions daily. Not all traders are day traders and some might be in the market for much longer periods.

Investing on the other hand is usually a longer-term proposition where shares or units might be held for many years. Similarly investing could be handed across to professional fund managers who invest of behalf of many clients.

## Money Beans Rule 6

*The market is cruel and doesn't care about you.*

The point of this rule is that going it alone might not be worth the risk. The "experts" have much more experience at it, usually. For many investors, (depending on time frame) a managed fund, or even an exchange traded fund could be a better bet. If you are young and have a long-time frame ahead of you – why not leave it to the experts? Set, forget and save. Remember, Einstein and compounding; you cannot have forgotten all ready?

Although a great strategy, many financial planners simply endorse savings plans with ETF's or Managed Funds (and I might agree as well), there is a certain pleasure in growing a portfolio with individual shares. Notwithstanding this, it's not for everyone. If you do decide it's for you, my suggestion (again, only general advice and whatever does not get me in trouble with the law keepers), is to get a paid newsletter subscription until you learn enough, and then still follow the paid subscription rather than go it alone. If you take the time to educate yourself well, then fair enough; go it alone. It's not an admission of defeat to use ETF's, though, by any degree. At least do something! And if it drops in value the next day, don't stress about it. If you are investing then this is a blip in the ocean. Generally, if you are investing for the long term, what happens the next day is of little consequence. If you are speculating, then that is a whole different feeling.

ETFs or exchange traded funds have a lower cost structure than the Managed Funds which are often part of banks or larger institutions.

They are a nimbler and more modern structure. Some might disagree, but they can. Other options when you have a larger sum to invest are SMA's or separately managed account which are shares held in your name, but not managed by you. What? It means for a fee a broker will buy and sell and make you money. Or not.

My advice is to steer clear of advice from those brokers who usually have other agendas. I am not saying their advice is necessarily poor, but sometimes it is biased – - remember *Money Beans Rules 2 and 13!*

What often happens is that the brokers have other corporate services that they perform for the companies they represent, that almost obligates them to make it seem desirable to advise you to buy their shares. It is really a conflict of interests although some might argue that they use their intimate knowledge of the company's strategies to put their would-be investors in a better place. Maybe, I am not sure.

Independent advice, on the other hand, from a newsletter type service, in which they make their recommendations based on their own research and opinions, albeit to sell newsletters, may be less biased and of higher quality. Part of the reason why this is so is that with poor recommendations they will soon go out of business.

This then makes them a better bet for many. You could then combine this paid advice with a low-cost broker, since the full advice brokers charge for their oftentimes biased advice far in excess of the low-cost brokers do, which means that if you trade often, the subscription becomes essentially free. Or you can find a decent full-service broker, and this can be a good choice depending on the amount of time, skill and desire to be involved that you have. They do often claim to have Chinese walls, which means although there may be an investment arm, they keep their business unknown to the dealers that are advising you. Do they? I don't know, again, maybe.

At this point, I can hear you saying, "What is he babbling about with the newsletters?"

Let's say that a subscription costs $1000 for a year, which could even be tax deductible, but forgetting that for now...

If you traded ten times in a year, and the full advice broker charged you $100 per trade, then you will pay $1000 in commissions. Brokerage is how they make money from you and it's on both the buy and the sell. Compare that to low-cost brokerage which might be $20 per trade then you will have paid only $100 in brokerage. If you subscribed to a newsletter for $500 then you would be $300 per year better off. This comparison just considers brokerage. Profits from rising prices is not considered.

Another way of looking at this is whilst you are building savings, perhaps the low-cost model is more suitable. The full cost broker won't have a lot of time for you anyway if your trade size is small.

**Events that can happen in the life of a share**

**Dividends**

*Dividends are good*

Dividends are a share of the profits of the company. Older people love dividends as they often may live off them since they provide income. As a younger person, you might be less interested and prefer that the company uses its profits to reinvest in its business and investors might invest in this type of share for its growth. I often look for a trade which has both. I do this not based on greed, rather, if one can pick up a 10% growth in share price followed by a 5% dividend, that is a nice trade. Compare that to the bank currently paying 0.25% interest.

Dividends depend on the company's profitability and finance needs but often, companies focus on growing profits and shareholders hope that their dividends grow accordingly. On the other hand, if the company grows and does not pay dividends, there is nothing stopping a shareholder selling some shares periodically if income is required. Just remember, there are tax consequences in doing that. Companies that focus on growth simply have different needs, and one is not better than another.

One of the few great things about the Australian tax system is imputation credits. Stay with me, this is good. Put simply it means that if the company pays tax on its profits, then the benefits of that tax payment transfers with the dividend. For example...

Depending on the tax bracket you are in, you could receive this $30

Shareholder receives a $100 dividend
(gross amount) with a $30 tax credit

credit back, or at least apply it to reduce the tax otherwise payable on the $100 deemed to have been received. More on this can be found on the ATO website.

If, for example, you earned $20,000 in a year and had a 20% tax rate, for discussion's sake, then the calculation is as follows:

Dividend income $100

Tax on dividend is 20% * 100 = $20

Less credit of $30

Means that a refund is due to you of $10

Within the realm of possibilities are fully franked dividends, partly franked dividends, and unfranked dividends.

This means if income is important to you then you have to compare the dividends on a grossed-up basis, but this is starting to get boring. It means that a 3% franked dividend might have more value to you, than a 3% unfranked dividend. In investment speak, dividends are "grossed up", by adding to the dividend amount the tax paid by the company on the profits from which the dividend was paid – i.e., the franking credit or imputed credit (both names mean the same thing).

**Company needs money**

Companies will, from time to time, need money. It is normal and nothing to worry about (unless, of course, it is purely to fund the Directors' lifestyles). They may choose to do this by issuing new shares rather than going to the bank. If they do, there are three main ways that this might be done:

1. Placement to institutional investors (Banks,insurance companies or fund managers usually). This means after, banks and companies that shares get issued (usually at a discount) to these investors and their friends. This is quick and can be cheaper to do than other methods, but means that the pie which was formerly 100 slices now has 120 slices. However, it also means that the company has more money. Often this can disadvantage existing and smaller shareholders.

2. Rights issue to shareholders. This may be offered according to the number of shares you, as a shareholder, have, or what is called pro-rata. For example, if the offer was 1 for 5 then for every five shares you own, you will be offered the chance to buy 1 new share at a certain set price. These offers can either be renounceable in which case you can sell the rights to the new shares, or non-renounceable which means you either take them up or not. There are lots of variations including the

ability to take up extra shares and share purchase plans.

3. Any combination of the above.

## Share splits and consolidations

"My shares are splitting?!" What is this all about? According to Investopedia, a stock split is a corporate action in which a company divides its existing shares into multiple shares to boost the liquidity of the shares. The primary motive is to make shares seem more affordable to small investors even though the underlying value of the company has not changed. Remember the pie, if there were ten slices and you had one, then if it is split to be ten times more you would have ten shares. You own the same percentage of the pie. If they were $10 before they would be $1 after. However, now, instead of owning one $10 share, you own ten $1 shares.

A consolidation is the reverse process, and might occur when the company is old and has issued billions of shares (yes, truly) which may now trade at cents. These so called "penny dreadful" stocks are great fun to trade sometimes, but, once again, I digress. After the consolidation they might end up with just some tens of millions of shares on issue, and trade at what seems like a more respectable price. Same pie, different perception. Perhaps before the shares traded at 0.5cents, and after they might trade at 50 cents.

## Suspension and de-listing

From time to time, the shares in a company may be suspended from trading. This can happen at a time when the Directors have something to announce that can affect the share price, and they want to maintain an informed market. The suspension serves to pause trading until that announcement can be made.

This is considered fair to everybody. The other reason for suspension is the company has been "a bit dodgy", or simply that the stock exchange considers the market to be poorly informed. Whatever the reason, it means that those shares you were going to make a fortune on cannot be traded online until the suspension is lifted. They can be traded off market if you can find a buyer, where the operative word is "if". All up, this isn't an ideal situation, and it can then only be resolved by the company releasing further and better, information after which its shares might be re-instated for trading.

A de-listing can occur if the company simply dies, gets taken over, or moves to another jurisdiction (as in another country most often). Taken over, simply means that another company buys all the shares and may offer shareholders shares in the new company or cash for the privilege or a combination of these.

**Share Registries**

In the olden days, companies had to issue share certificates. They were numbered and had the shareholders' name on them. Shareholders were required to deliver them to their stock broker if they wanted to sell them. The share registry is the place where these records now kept and they would issue a new share certificate to the person who purchased the shares. They also send the original shareholder notices and organise dividends. They still do this but now it's mostly electronic and you, as a present-day shareholder, won't get a certificate any more. Instead, you will get one of these wonderful documents which is a confirmation of registration. The broker will also issue a confirmation of trade which serves as a record for brokerage (fees) as well.

# Beach Energy Limited
ABN: 20 007 617 969
Place of Incorporation/Registration: SA

| Holder ID Number (HIN): | |
|---|---|
| CHESS Sponsor's ID (PID): | 01402 |
| Statement Period: | November 2020 |
| Page: | 1 of 1 |

### BPT - ORDINARY FULLY PAID

| Date | Transaction Type | Transaction ID | Ex/Cum Status | Quantity On | Off | Holding Balance |
|---|---|---|---|---|---|---|
| 03 Nov 20 | Movement of Securities due to Purchase, Sale or Transfer | 0140220938549000 | | 10000 | | 10000 |

**FOR YOUR INFORMATION**

☛ To obtain full terms and conditions of an Issuer's securities contact the Issuer's Registrar or the Issuer directly.
☛ For information about CHESS Depositary Interests (CDIs) and to obtain a free copy of the Financial Services Guide (FSG) or any supplementary FSG for CHESS Depositary Nominees Pty Ltd go to www.asx.com.au/cdis or phone 131 279.
☛ ASX Settlement may by law need to disclose information in CHESS Holdings to third parties.

*Refer overleaf for additional important information*

Share Registry Details:

**ASX**

Issued By:
ASX Settlement Pty Limited | ABN 49 008 504 532 | PO Box H227, Australia Square, Sydney NSW 1215

# All about Loans and Gearing

Just saying that the views that I express here are all my own, for better or worse. Although I am at the time of writing, a Liberty adviser, the views in this book are neither endorsed by Liberty, nor approved by Liberty in any way shape or form. This simply means that I have my own way of delivering content that might be inconsistent with Liberty's way of delivering similar information. These are my views based on my experience, and sense of humour and that is that.

**Negative gearing can be bad.**

Through the growth phase along the journey to a little wealth, you might choose to legally minimise the tax that you pay by borrowing for investment purposes. This is called gearing and can be either positive or negative. In the finance world, gearing has nothing to do with the gears we know from vehicle world, but is instead just a fancy word for borrowing.

Stay with me. Check this out.

Say Joan had an investment property which earned her $20,000 per year, but cost her $10,000 in interest. This is positive gearing, because she earns more than it costs her, and the difference of $10,000 would get added to her income from working to arrive at her taxable income for the year. If that same property cost her $30,000 in interest per year then this would mean that she was negatively geared, and that negative amount would decrease her taxable income for the year.

Many accountants love to see this and I was no different. It is not illegal; it can be beneficial but also financially disastrous if things don't turn out. While it can magnify the benefits, it equally magnifies the losses, if things change, and they can!

## Home Loans

There are many different house loans available and many more products, where products are a bundle of facilities and potential benefits offered by the various lenders in the markets. Canstar, for example, assesses over 4,000 products. I am not sure about you, but I would certainly struggle to be able to assess that many, even though I am a mortgage broker. It is simply not viable if every time someone wants a loan to scan through that many different options. That is why I, like so many others, have a panel of lenders to work from and the software to assess what is best for my customers. My duty as a broker is to do what's best for my customer and not what is best for me.

Besides the fact that there are rules, it is inherently obvious to anyone with the right ethics that this is the case. I can only wonder at how those institutions that only offer their own products meet with this obligation, but they don't have to; go figure. But more about home loans. For most people, a home is the single largest investment they will make. Hopefully for you, readers, it will not be, but then you are not most people.

## Boring stats

*Own your own home if you can.*

Because the majority of us don't have a spare million or two just sitting around, we need to borrow large sums of money if we want to buy our own home. Lots of people don't mind renting, but I will admit that I am not one of them. According to the Australian Bureau of Statistics, though, increasing numbers of households are renting. "The proportion of Australian households renting their home increased to 32 per cent in 2017–18, according to new figures released by the Australian Bureau of Statistics (ABS). This is an increase from 27 per cent in 1997–98.

Over the same 20-year period, the proportion of households that rented their home from a private landlord increased to 27 per cent (up from 20 per cent), while the proportion of public housing tenants decreased from 6 per cent to 3 per cent.

"Most of the increase in renter households was in the private rental market," said ABS Chief Economist, Bruce Hockman. "Some of the decrease in public housing numbers can be attributed to recent trends in social housing provision which have seen the community housing sector taking on an increasingly prominent role."

The proportion of households that owned their own home fell to 66 per cent, down from 70 per cent in 1997-98. The proportion of households that owned their home without a mortgage decreased to 30 per cent (down from 40 per cent), while the proportion who owned their home with a mortgage increased to 37 per cent (up from 31 per cent).

One in five households (20 per cent) owned one or more residential properties other than their usual residence. Of those households that owned other residential property, 71 per cent owned a single property, while 5 per cent owned four or more properties.

Housing costs remained steady for most household tenure types when compared to recent years. On average, in 2017-18, renters paid $366 per week on housing, while housing costs for owners with a mortgage were $484 per week.

"Interest rates have remained relatively low over the past several years and we have seen a recent softening in the rental market in some major cities," Mr. Hockman also said.

The data shows that renters continued to devote more of their income to housing than home owners. On average, private renters paid 20 per cent of their income on housing costs, compared to 16 per cent for owners with a mortgage and 3 per cent for households who owned their home outright.

Lower income households spent a greater proportion of their household income on housing. On average, lower income households renting privately paid $339 per week which was 32 per cent of their gross weekly income. Lower income households who owned their home with a mortgage paid on average $376 per week which was 29 per cent of their gross weekly income.

**I know it's boring, but I did warn you.**

The average Australian home loan for March 2018 was $388,100 according to the Australian Bureau of Statistics (ABS). That is a lot of money, and it does vary depending on where you live.

- New South Wales: $445,500
- Victoria: $400,200
- Queensland: $341,700
- South Australia: $311,300
- Western Australia: $343,900
- Tasmania: $252,100
- Northern Territory: $309,400
- Australian Capital Territory: $383,000

So, hello Tassie!

The message should be clear hopefully, that if you want to avoid paying off someone else's mortgage (aka renting), and, since this is a very large investment, getting it right with the right terms and conditions ought to be important to you. Make sure you are getting the right advice and choose an adviser who can explain things to you well.

So, this home loan thing is all about borrowing a bucketload of money to get a house. The expectation is that the house will grow in value and you are borrowing to finance an asset that increases in value every year forever. Reality is not always quite as ideal, and although proponents of real estate will show you glowing graphs of growth that lasts forever, do your research and follow *Money Beans Rules 2,3, and 4*.

Additionally, buy well; don't fall in love with a property and understand what renovation costs might be if you are not building. More on building later.

Having said what I said, most people ignore advice and go and buy what they want. I can't control that, but I can try to pass on some knowledge.

**What is the Home Buying Process and what other costs are there?**

Homes are either new or used, just like cars. But unlike most cars, they can be built to your specifications, but for many home buyers are just off the plan as offered. Basically, if you want to change to many anything, it will cost you more. For your first home, (if you are building) I suggest (without recommending) that you take what is offered as is it is usually the cheapest way forward. There are often house and land packages where the builders and land developers each make lots of money but do provide an opportunity for you to get started.

Beware though, that the house they will sell you is not a home. That is, most basic home packages offer specifications that will form the shell of your house, but to make it a home, you will need to factor in other elements. These might, include landscaping (unless you like a sand pit), curtains (unless you like entertaining the neighbours), and perhaps fans or air conditioner depending on your environment (unless you're the breed of human who enjoys 44-degree days). All I am saying is you get a shell depending on what enticements are being offered. Bottom line, first home buyers, don't go crazy and just take what is offered, as it is often the cheapest. You can do changes in future years without having to borrow too much money now.

With any home there are other costs, apart from purchase. For example, stamp duty is a tax that is charged by all Australian states and territories on property purchases. This amount is based on the property purchase price, location and loan purpose. This means that the stamp duty price might vary if the property or home you're buying is for residence or an investment. With a new house, usually the stamp duty will apply to just the land. First home buyers also get concessions depending on which state you live in.

Since you know I like examples by now, consider the following that may apply for a house in Western Australia valued at $400,000: -

These were current at 1 June 2020, figures may change, etc; you know the rest.

| | First Home Buyer | Non first home buyer |
|---|---|---|
| Mortgage registration fee | 171 | 171 |
| Transfer fee | 241 | 241 |
| Stamp Duty | 0 | 13,015 |

Back to the process. If you buy a new home then you have to make a lot of decisions from carpets to taps to elevations. Elevations are views of what the house looks like as opposed to floor plans which just show the layout! You can start to get an idea of what it will look like and sometimes 3D walk throughs are possible. For someone with as much imagination as me, a display home works better to give a sense of room sizes and space.

It can be exhausting or exhilarating, that depends on you. But don't forget to allow money for the extras and get some quotes for everything else you want, before you decide. Then you get to sign a contract so you need to have finance arranged. A lender will want to see the contract and make sure that you are getting a complete home since, if for some reason you stop paying, they want to be in a position to sell a complete, and not a half-built, house.

During the construction period, you will be charged progressively, or your loan account will, depending on the lender, and various progress payments will be made to the builder based on milestone achievements, like the slab being poured. Once handover has occurred, then all payments from the bank to the builder should have been made; congratulations, you now have your home, and your mortgage.

**What is a mortgage?**

A mortgage is a legal term, the meaning of which is that in exchange for a lender lending you money, the lender takes security over your house and land. This means that if you are unable or unwilling to make your repayments, the bank has the right to sell your house (yes, out you go), and recoup not only what they are owed, but the sale costs, and any repairs they deem necessary to put the house into saleable condition. This could include a bunch of other costs such that you absolutely never want to be in this position.

You may have come across the term "mortgagee in possession" which means someone defaulted and the mortgagee (the lender), now is running the show. Not only will you get a bad credit record, you will pay for many people to have a role in selling your pride and joy. How do you avoid this? Don't borrow beyond your means and be sensible. Oh yes, and make sure you pay regularly and on time.

Other costs of buying a house include a settlement agent or solicitor. They organise and synchronise the exchange of money with the registration of title (fancy name for who owns the land), as well as notifying institutions like Water Corporation and the local Council that you are the new owners, and for them to start charging you for water, rates etc. They act on your behalf to ensure you are buying what you think you are buying and everyone knows who the new owners are. Items like rates and taxes are adjusted which means, because they are charged annually and usually paid by the previous owner, you might owe them for a portion of what they paid since they will no longer be there.

You will get a settlement statement which will look something like this.

# SETTLEMENT STATEMENT

## FINAL SETTLEMENT STATEMENT

| | |
|---|---|
| Client: | Mr and Mrs MoneyBeans |
| Property: | 7 Magical Crescent, Woop Woop |
| Settlement Date: | 20 July 2020 |

| | Debit | Credit |
|---|---|---|
| Purchase price | $590,000.00 | |
| Less deposit paid | | $10,000.00 |
| Transfer duty (General Rate) | $24,300.00 | |
| Landgate - Transfer registration fee | $284.70 | |
| PEXA fee | $114.07 | |
| Settlement fees and disbursements (see schedule) | $1,479.29 | |
| **Rates Apportionment as at 20 April 2020** | | |
| 1. City of Woop Woop rates 2019-20: not yet raised<br>Your estimated share | $400.00 | |
| 2. Water rates 1/3/20 to 30/4/20: not yet raised<br>Your estimated share | $50.00 | |
| 3. Land tax 2019-20: $955.50<br>Your share (71/366 days) | $185.36 | |
| Total funds required for settlement | | $606,813.42 |

It shows all the movements in funds including your purchase, your deposit, and a bunch of fees and adjustments for services like water and rates. Since rates and paid in advance, the seller wants their share back!

You will also need to organise power and gas (unless you like camping, in which case a tent is much cheaper!). You must also arrange to have the house insured before settlement and usually you name the lender, as what is called an interested party. They have a huge interest since that is their security. Don't save money on cheap insurance. This is a major investment. This is a time for quality. Oops that was advice. Warning, common sense happens.

At the risk of being accused of being repetitive, with a new home, particularly a first home buyer has to consider the finishes. When budgeting for your new home, buyers need to understand that what a builder says as being finished does not necessarily equate to liveable. It simply means they have finished with the build and are ready to hand over the keys. So, you need to understand the details of what they are supplying, so you are not caught short.

You therefore may need to budget for some or all of these, depending on your contract: -

- Interior painting
- Light fittings
- Floor coverings
- Paving
- Driveway
- Crossover
- Landscaping and reticulation
- Curtains and blinds
- Ongoing insurance
- Security screens
- Security system
- Air-conditioning

These can add up, so don't spend every last dollar without thinking about these items.

## Different Types of Home Loans

Lenders make money by borrowing at one rate and then lending it to you at a higher rate. Nice business! Someone has to pay for their lavish offices, and that is you and anyone else wanting money, but that is the way of the world. At least when there are capital gains to be made, the lender does not ask for a share of that!

Interest rates are essentially the cost of borrowing and often in the loan agreement will refer to a base rate of interest that you will be charged over the life of the loan and the total interest to be paid is an amount calculated over the life, or term of the loan. Okay, so far?

The main types of loans are interest only, and principal and interest. There are also fixed and variable rates of interest.

With an interest only loan, say you borrowed $250,000 for five years. At the end of the five years you still owe $250,000 but have paid interest during the term (life) of the loan.

In a principal and interest loan, eventually you start to nibble away at the principal (which is the amount of money you borrowed to buy your dream home). An example will help. Yes, another example, but it does make it clearer.

If you took a loan of, say, $250,000 at an interest rate of 3% for a thirty-year period (the term), and assuming you made monthly repayments, then the repayment schedule might look like this:

| Pmt No. | Payment Date | Beginning Balance | Payment | Principal | Interest | Ending Balance |
|---|---|---|---|---|---|---|
| 1 | 1/8/20 | $250,000.00 | $1,054.01 | $429.01 | $625.00 | $249,570.99 |
| 2 | 1/9/20 | $249,570.99 | $1,054.01 | $430.08 | $623.93 | $249,140.91 |
| 3 | 1/10/20 | $249,140.91 | $1,054.01 | $431.16 | $622.85 | $248,709.75 |
| 4 | 1/11/20 | $248,709.75 | $1,054.01 | $432.24 | $621.77 | $248,277.51 |
| 5 | 1/12/20 | $248,277.51 | $1,054.01 | $433.32 | $620.69 | $247,844.20 |
| 6 | 1/1/21 | $247,844.20 | $1,054.01 | $434.40 | $619.61 | $247,409.80 |
| 7 | 1/2/21 | $247,409.80 | $1,054.01 | $435.49 | $618.52 | $246,974.31 |
| 8 | 1/3/21 | $246,974.31 | $1,054.01 | $436.57 | $617.44 | $246,537.74 |
| 9 | 1/4/21 | $246,537.74 | $1,054.01 | $437.67 | $616.34 | $246,100.07 |
| 10 | 1/5/21 | $246,100.07 | $1,054.01 | $438.76 | $615.25 | $245,661.31 |
| 11 | 1/6/21 | $245,661.31 | $1,054.01 | $439.86 | $614.15 | $245,221.46 |
| 12 | 1/7/21 | $245,221.46 | $1,054.01 | $440.96 | $613.05 | $244,780.50 |
| 13 | 1/8/21 | $244,780.50 | $1,054.01 | $442.06 | $611.95 | $244,338.44 |
| 14 | 1/9/21 | $244,338.44 | $1,054.01 | $443.16 | $610.85 | $243,895.28 |
| 15 | 1/10/21 | $243,895.28 | $1,054.01 | $444.27 | $609.74 | $243,451.00 |

On the first line you can see your beginning balance which is the loan amount of $250,000. The next column shows a constant monthly payment and the next two columns break up that amount between principal repayments and interest. Being the observant person, you are by now; you will see that the principal month by month increases and the interest decreases. So much so, by payment 15, the principal, or amount owing is now $243,895. Okay, and 28 cents!

Summing up, it looks like the graph below. Eventually, you owe nothing. Happy days!

Time runs along the horizontal axis and equals the loan term. (30 years).

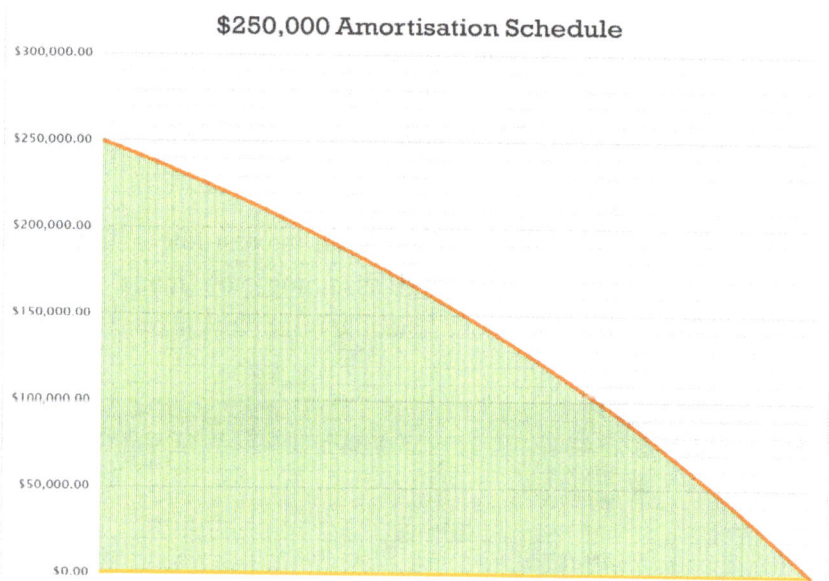

$250,000 Amortisation Schedule

## Other factors with loans

### Variable vs Fixed rate

As well as which type of loan you could take out, you also need to consider which type of interest rate you want. Here, there are two options; a variable rate or a fixed rate.

What does that mean? Well, I'll explain.

A fixed rate loan means that for an agreed period (often 1-5 years), the rate won't change. It is, well, fixed. After that, it often reverts to a variable rate loan. Now, that means what? It means that the bank, in response to movements in the base rates, which are in turn set by the Reserve Bank, will amend your loan's rate of interest.

Say on day one, the variable rate was 3%. If one month later, the Reserve Bank announces that the base rate was to increase by 0.25%, then your lender will send you a nice letter to say that your repayments will increase and the rate of interest you will pay in future will increase by an amount often equal to more or less the increase stated by the Reserve Bank. The same happens when rates decrease and the savings will pass on to you. See how to save money, though, in the exciting section to follow.

This is the sort of fascinating announcement that they make.

Media Release

## Statement by Philip Lowe, Governor: Monetary Policy Decision

Number    **2020-01**

Date      **4 February 2020**

At its meeting today, the Board decided to leave the cash rate unchanged at 0.75 per cent.

The outlook for the global economy remains reasonable. There have been signs that the slowdown in global growth that started in 2018 is coming to an end. Global growth is expected to be a little stronger this year and next than it was last year and inflation remains low almost everywhere. One continuing source of uncertainty, despite recent progress, is the trade and technology dispute between the US and China, which has affected international trade flows and investment. Another source of uncertainty is the coronavirus, which is having a significant effect on the Chinese economy at present. It is too early to determine how long-lasting the impact will be.

Interest rates are very low around the world and a number of central banks eased monetary policy over the second half of last year. There is an expectation of a little further monetary easing in some economies. Long-term government bond yields are around record lows in many countries, including Australia. Borrowing rates for both businesses and households are at historically low levels. The Australian dollar is around its lowest level over recent times.

## How to Cheat the Banks

I can hear you saying, "You can't say that". Well, I did. The bank exists to make money for its shareholders and to maintain its coffers to lend to the next person and the next. There are some that may claim societal benefits but they are often more likely to be found in Europe than Australia. Perhaps some of the smaller institutions, like credit unions, have more of a heart. So, when I say cheat, don't worry – I don't mean anything unethical or illegal and would, in fact, strongly advise (and this is where I can give advice) you don't go down a path of lawbreaking. Rather, what I mean is just figure out how can you turn the tables a little more in your favour. Sound good? Read on.

### Keep repaying the same amount if the rates drop

When interest rates drop, your minimum repayments might go from, for example's sake, $250 per week to $230 per week, immediately saving you a nice $80 every month ($20 a week for 4 weeks).

What if, though, when rates dropped, you kept your repayments at the same amount? After all, with the above example, you could afford it to make that extra $20 per week payment last month. If you maintain the same rate of payment you will repay your principal faster. This is a good thing and so that is one option.

### Pay more frequently

The other option, if your lender permits, is to increase the frequency of payment so instead of paying monthly, you make payments weekly or fortnightly. This can make a large difference over a longer period, but you need to check that this will give you an advantage.

If we use our $250,000 loan mentioned previously, then you could save some interest by paying more frequently because interest is usually calculated based on a daily compounding rate, even though you might pay monthly. For instance, if in one month you made two fortnightly payments of $1,000 instead of one monthly payment of

$2,000 on a $250,000 balance, you'd be accruing interest on $250,000 for one half of the month and $249,000 for the rest of the month – as opposed to being charged interest on $250,000 over the whole month.

By paying more frequently, it will actually mean that you could pay less overall.

It also might suit your cash flow better if you were paid weekly for example.

**What about lump sum repayments?**

A lump sum payment is simply where you may might have a windfall and rather than buying a nice new motorcycle, decide to pay a lump sum off your home loan. It could be a good idea on your journey to that happy place called No More Home Loan! It could also be that you had saved up and don't need the money right now Some loans permit a redraw, but not all. Check with your friendly mortgage broker.

**Other bits and pieces to do with Home Loans**

Loans are all the same, right? Well, no, not exactly, and this is why a mortgage broker, like myself, can offer some help and guidance to walk you through the process and get you the most suitable loan for your circumstances. Yes, that was a shameless bit of advertising but I do offer a service that can provide you with the best options and if you've read this far, I can only imagine we'd get along. In saying that, I'd still always advise you recall *Money Beans Rule No 13*.

---

## Money Beans Rule 13

---

*Be careful who you trust:*

The be careful who you trust is a part of the rule and shoudl be in italiscs like the other rules here are some different features of loans to consider, apart from the fixed vs variable interest rates and principal and interest or interest only.

**Package rates**: There are often packages that attract an annual fee, in return for a bundle of services like a credit card you may not need, a discount on standard interest rates and no monthly fees. But you have to realise that the annual fee is monthly fees paid 12 months at once, so do you really benefit?

**Basic loan**: No frills, but no fees. Often, these are all you may need, but you need to know such things exist in the first place. Sometimes the terms and conditions are not as flexible as standard loans, but not always.

**Split accounts**: This is something best spoken to your financial adviser about, but means you might have a portion of your loan split into fixed and another into variable rates. Similarly, you may have one loan with different split accounts for different purposes, like investing or similar. For most people, and particularly first home buyers, you will not likely need these extras.

**Offset accounts**: These might be useful to save you some interest. It involves you parking some money in an account that earns little to no interest, and the loan is treated as being reduced by that amount, meaning that therefore a lower interest rate applies. Since you probably don't have a lazy $100,000, I am not sure how valuable this may be to you, but it's a thing nonetheless, (and again, a mortgage broker should be able to advise you).

**Extra repayments**: The ability to make extra repayments is a useful feature to have, and most lenders permit this.

**Redraw**: The ability to borrow again using the same loan (usually limited to the amount of the original loan).

**Serviceability**: means you can afford the repayments. In years gone by, loans were sometimes issued in circumstances where the borrower might have been better counselled not to have borrowed, as they simply could not afford it. As a consequence, there have been umpteen

Royal Commissions and enquiries and now there is much more scrutiny of expenses to try and make sure that the borrower is able to afford the loan. This in itself is not a bad thing, but means the process is slower and can be frustrating for the seemingly never-ending requirement to produce documents. Different lenders stress the repayments to determine serviceability which means that although the current rate might be say 3% they see if the borrower can afford to repay if rates rose to 5%.

It is my view, and not shared by all, that people often borrow too much and set themselves up for unnecessary hardship. An example would be committing heavily right now in a low interest rate regime, where you can *just* afford repayments on your loan. While it's awesome from a borrower perspective that interest rates are so low, what happens if interest rates rise and with each announcement from the RBA, go up? You have to ask yourself if, under changing circumstances, you would still be able to repay your loan. If you couldn't, it will likely be bye-bye lattes; or worse, bye-bye house.

This is why you have to be careful to draw the line between taking advantage of a good situation, and letting a too-good situation take advantage of you.

Now, if we revisit the previous example, our $250,000 loan demands the following principal and interest monthly repayments at the following differing interest rates.

| Interest | Monthly Repayment |
|:---:|:---:|
| 3% | $1,054 |
| 3.5% | $1,123 |
| 4% | $1,193 |
| 4.5% | $1,267 |

According to Trading Economics, the interest rate in Australia averaged 4.22 percent from 1990 until 2020, reaching an all-time high of 17.50 percent in January of 1990 and a record low of 0.25 percent in March of 2020. So, committing to the maximum now, might not be super smart; unless you expect your income to rise by a greater amount. It depends where you are on the treadmill of life. I recall the higher rates all too well, and it was difficult.

**Other Types of Loans**

**Personal Loans**

Personal loans can be a lifeline or a pathway to despair. Like any loan, they are relatively easy to get but attract higher interest rates, because they are unsecured. Loans that are secured – for instance, by the equity in your house, can be obtained at lower rates because they are simply lower risk. When I first started off in my own home, I had no spare cash, so I went off to the local bank and came back with $1,000 – enough to buy some really nasty second-hand furniture and a washing machine and fridge, but I was as happy as could be.

That loan was able to be paid back in a short time as I had income and all was well with the world. Getting a head start is a good reason to take out a loan, combined with a short repayment period and an income being more than enough to make the repayments. Borrowing more and more is not ever a recipe for success.

Other reasons you might want to take a loan includes for a wedding, a holiday, some urgent medical expenses, or even renovations. Good reasons, ability to repay quickly, and not have any financial stress in the meantime all get the Money Beans tick of approval. Overloading yourself financially, does not. If it is truly unavoidable, then maybe. If it is for just a splurge then unless you can easily manage the repayments, it is not the best course of action. "Oh, but this so nice and new! Those $500 shoes are so nice! I need a new PlayStation." Yeah, yeah. But not worth getting into financial stress for.

## Refinancing

Refinancing, or "refi" as it's affectionately called, is a fantastic opportunity to reduce debt. Imagine you did not have this book, and ended up with a bunch of debt, all with high interest rates. Naturally, you are struggling to make payments, and life is not that great anymore. The repayments last long after whatever pleasure you might have thought was important. Refinancing, at this point, can be a lifeline that will help.

Refinancing is a way to make this burden easier. Depending on your circumstances you might be able to do something like this:

Let's say you have a number of credit cards, and owe $25,000 with an average interest rate of 18%. Often it can be more than this, but play along with me....

Say you are managing to pay $700 per month. That is quite a lot, but maybe you feel it is okay, as you're getting by.

But what if you could make your life better by refinancing? The process is simple enough. Fees and charges apply, and lending criteria of course, but this is where the magic happens in this example.

If you could refinance your loans even with a $1500 fee, then by refinancing your current loan balance of $25,000.00 at 8% over 5 years, you would decrease your monthly payments by $193.09 and add just 8 months to the loan term. The total interest you would pay over the life of the new loan would decrease by $5,659.76. You would even recoup the fees associated with refinancing your loan after just 8 months!

|  | Current Loan | Refinanced loan |
|---|---|---|
| Monthly Payment | $700.00 | $506.91 |
| Total Payments | $36,074.38 | $30,414.62 |
| Total Interest | $11,074.38 | $5,414.62 |
| Pay-off Date | Octobe 28, 2024 | June 28, 2025 |

Not only would have you saved interest, you have reduced the amount of money you need to find each month. Once you have done this, get out the scissors and say bye to those credit cards.

## Car Loans

There is nothing like a shiny new car. When you're looking to purchase, you will be given all the reasons why buying a new car is the best idea in the world, and that you're getting the best deal of the century. However, don't forget, that the moment you leave the lot, your brand new, swanky car has lost at least 10% of its value. The moment it rains, it looks the same as a second-hand car. There might be a time for a new car, later on when you have lots of spare money, but at the beginning of your sudden responsible-ness is not that time.

It is also good to shop around for a car loan, and I might be able to help, but for new cars although it looks like the dealer's finance is great, you should be cautious of, these "attractive" offers. Often you can negotiate a better purchase price by arranging finance elsewhere, which means your repayments may be less. This is because, it might be based, on a lower purchase price.

# Payday Loans

These are evil. They are short term loans with very high rates, repayable on, you guess it... payday. If you follow my plan of putting aside for a rainy day, you will never need these. They look bad on your credit report if you are late, and needing these means you have not followed the Money Beans plan so, shame on you! According to Moneystart, lenders can't charge interest on payday loans, but they can charge a lot in fees. You will have to pay back a lot more than you borrowed. Most payday lenders charge an establishment fee of 20% of the amount borrowed and a monthly service fee of 4% of the amount borrowed. Bad, bad, bad; don't do it. In case you are reaching for a calculator, let me save you the trouble – that is 48%, plus the establishment fee. Did I mention that I don't like them?

# Buy Now, Pay Later

There are many of these cards, including Afterpay and ZIP. They offer you the chance to make split payments (four) with no interest. If you pay on time, the only one who pays for the service technically is the merchant. There are variations and they could be a good way to manage cash flows. This is, of course, is based on you making payments on time. If you're late, then it's penalty interest time. You will be all but eaten alive with interest and fees.

One way you could manage this is to use your internet banking to make automatic payments. No forgetting, and not a bad way of taking a small fee and interest free loan. One thing to be aware of is the view of lenders. If you have a bunch of these then a lender may form a view that you are living beyond your means so, be aware. Perception is their reality!

I wonder also if you approached the merchant and asked for the price without using a buy now pay later method of payment, whether you might get a better price?

## Putting Your Best Foot Forward

When you apply for a home loan, it is a lot of money, and the lender wants to make sure you are the right sort of person who can manage such responsibility. Whilst this is their business, and they do it regularly, they really want to avoid defaults and having to repossess your home, so they make all the checks they reasonably can.

They want to see that you are stable (well, financially anyway) ☺. That means not changing address regularly, or jobs. It means they want a decent credit report on you which reveals no defaults, no legal actions and no record of late payments. Some lending institutions are more understanding than others but it is really important for you to manage repayments well, if not perfectly. Although there are some lenders that are more understanding, even so it comes at a cost to you by having to pay higher interest rate.

If you have a few credit cards, then get rid of them. Maybe keep one with a low limit. If you have a credit issue, your mortgage broker may have someone who can help clean up your record for a fee. If you do have a number of loans including credit card debt, consider refi (sounds like Mexican takeaway, doesn't it?). See earlier for more information on this.

Payday loans, regular gambling, and lots of late payments are all warning signs to lenders. These may disqualify you from the lower cost options. Sometimes, though, these are other options which do not need as much documentation and (called low doc loans for a reason), in return for the higher risk to the lender, you pay a higher rate of interest. If it can be the means to an end then it could be worth it as you don't have to stay with any lender for the full term of the loan. You might even find after say, two years of good behaviour and regular payments, you could look for a better rate. More reasons to work with a good mortgage broker. (Shameless ad goes here).

# Insurance

There are lots of different insurances. The ones most likely to affect you, if you're suddenly responsible at a young age include car, health, home and contents, and maybe for your jet-ski or other expensive equipment if you have any. As you get older and become perhaps even more responsible (i.e., you have dependents), then you may need to consider life insurance or some of the trauma covers. There is also income protection insurance that you can consider.

All the Money Beans rules apply to insurances as well.

Things you need to know about insurance include:

- Duty to disclose – if you don't tell them everything they could reasonably want to know; you may have no cover at all

- If you are drunk, your vehicle may not be covered

- If your vehicle has been modified and they don't know, you may have no cover

- If you have had a prior illness that is relevant, you may not have cover

- If you are negligent in your property maintenance, your cover may be reduced

Some insurances require an excess to be chosen by you. This is the amount you would pay in the event of a claim. For example, if you had a property with a $500 excess and some damage was caused to it with repairs costing $5000, you would only receive back $4,500 as you will have to pay your excess amounting to $500. You might get the chance to choose a higher or lower excess when you take the policy out. In doing so, it means the premium, which is your upfront cost for a period of cover, will go up or down respectively (note: your premium will go up if you choose a lower excess and vice versa).

The following is a guide. I am not qualified to advise you, but at least you might know the basics of how to start.

**Where to Buy Insurance?**

*Choose quality over price but choose something!*

You can buy it online, you could use a broker, or you could use comparison services to get you started. These might help you choose. (I like Canstar, but have a hunt around).

Even though a broker will charge you a fee, they will also give you advice. They will also know which insurers are good to work with. The comparison sites often get a fee from the companies, so choose independence, and shop around.

**Motor Vehicle Insurance**

If you purchase a motor vehicle, then some insurance is compulsory and built into your cost of registration.

Compulsory third party (CTP) insurance is a minimum level of cover in Australia. You automatically get CTP insurance in WA, when you pay your car registration. CTP covers you against personal injury you might cause to another person in a car accident or incident.

This means that you're covered if you're held responsible for any injuries or fatalities to third parties caused in an accident. This is a good thing to be included and gives you that peace of mind that someone you may injure will at least be cared for. However, CTP does not cover damage to cars, vehicles or property you may destroy or any injury you suffer as a consequence. This means if you are responsible for an accident, you could be liable for many thousands of dollars of damage to other cars or property if you only have CTP insurance. Just imagine if you ploughed into someone's house.

You might want to consider additional insurance to give you extra cover, and if it is a new car, you definitely might sleep better knowing it is well covered. If not, you may be paying off a loan for something that is no longer drivable, if it is a write-off.

## Third party car insurance

Third party car insurance covers you for damage, legal costs and repairs to other (third party) vehicles or property in an accident. Third party car insurance still though does not cover you for the cost of repairs or replacement for your own car, or the cost of replacing your car if it gets stolen.

Third party insurance might possibly include uninsured driver cover, so if you're in an accident with an uninsured driver who is at fault, repairs to your car could be covered up to a limit.

## Third party with fire and theft

Third party fire and theft is a level higher than third party car insurance, and this level of insurance will cover damage to your car caused by fire or theft. Some insurers even include uninsured driver cover, which means if you're involved in an accident with an uninsured driver and the uninsured driver is at fault, repairs to your car could be covered up to a limit.

## Comprehensive car insurance

Comprehensive car insurance is the highest level of car insurance cover. It should include:

- Repair and replacement of your car due to fire, theft, malicious damage, accidental damage and weather-related damage.

- Repair and replacement of any other vehicles or property that are damaged by your car in an accident.

Comprehensive car insurance covers you for the cost of repairs regardless of who is responsible for the damage. It costs more than other types of insurance, but gives you the most protection. Some car finance loans require comprehensive car insurance as a condition of the loan.

## Vehicle Equity Insurance

Even though you might have comprehensive insurance on your car, if it is written off, there may be a shortfall. What? How can that be? Well for a number of reasons. A gap can arise because of any of the following:

- Excess that applied on your comprehensive cover.

- Registration fees on the next vehicle.

- New vehicle comprehensive insurance on the next vehicle

- Stamp duty and dealer delivery on the next vehicle.

## Bicycle Insurance

It is possible to get very affordable bicycle insurance from RAC which is interesting because you have to consider that this is a vehicle on the road and, even if covered as part of your contents, it is unlikely that the cover would, extend to the consequences of an accident. This particular policy includes:

- Accidental loss or damage

- Other people riding your bike

- Cover for fire and theft

- Includes accessories

- Legal liability (personal or property)

Check out https://rac.com.au/home-life/bike-insurance to find out more.

## House Insurance

This is most likely your biggest insurable asset apart from perhaps your income; and oh yeah, your life. The main thing here is to make sure you do your sums carefully, as there is a horrible thing called co-insurance that you should avoid. What this means is, if you don't insure for enough, the insurer can assume you were sharing the risk and will only cover you for their share. Sucks? It can but as long as you don't underinsure, you won't have to worry. Insurance companies usually offer all sorts of calculators to help you get to the correct figure of what to insure your house for, which could include things like temporary accommodation and taking away the rubbish. These are all things that you don't want to think about, but can make a bad situation more bearable.

As well as the house, there are your contents to think about. Phrases like "new for old" are important to understand. This means if you lose your old something, you get a new something. Note that when it comes to contents, there are contents in the house and contents outside your house (like a laptop). You have to decide what you want to cover and whether it is worth it.

House and contents policies can be tailored to suit different circumstances which might include;

- You whilst you are renting – generally contents only

- You as a homeowner including the building, its contents and sometime public liability which covers someone else at your home

- Just contents, for whatever reason

- Landlord insurance to provide for damage and loss of rent

- Specialist body corporate insurance

- All risks insurance – for your valuables whilst travelling

- Building insurance – for when you are, well, building.

## Personal Insurances

These cover you or your family and include private health insurance, life insurance, income protection insurance, trauma insurance and travel insurance. Well, these are the main ones you will come across.

## Health Insurance

*Health insurance is cheaper when you are young and might avoid an additional Medicare Levy.*

Medical Benefits, comprises hospital and medical covers in usually a combined policy. Whilst Medibank covers some expenses, it does not cover everything and means you might have to wait a long time to get the treatment you would get quicker if insured. The Australian Government offers health insurance rebate to offset the cost.

**Warning; the following is boring and just included for completeness.**

Most Australians with private health insurance currently receive a rebate from the Australian Government to help cover the cost of their premiums. The private health insurance rebate is income tested. The table below details the different rebate amounts and Medicare Levy Surcharge levels. The private health insurance rebate is an amount the government contributes towards the cost of your private hospital health insurance premiums.

The rebate applies to hospital treatment, general treatment and ambulance policies. It does not apply to overseas visitors health cover. The rebate levels applicable from 1 April 2019 to 31 March 2021* are:

| Singles<br>Families | ≤$90,000<br>≤$180,000 | $90,001-105,000<br>$180,001-210,000 | $105,001-140,000<br>$210,001-280,000 | ≥$140,001<br>≥$280,001 |
|---|---|---|---|---|
| | | Rebate | | |
| | Base Tier | Tier 1 | Tier 2 | Tier 3 |
| < age 65 | 25.059% | 16.706% | 8.352% | 0% |
| Age 65-69 | 29.236% | 20.883% | 12.529% | 0% |
| Age 70+ | 33.413% | 25.059% | 16.706% | 0% |

Single parents and couples (including de facto couples) are subject to family tiers. For families with children, the income thresholds are increased by $1,500 for each child after the first. The income thresholds are indexed and will remain the same to 30 June 2021.

The above is a bit complicated, so here is a link to a calculator kindly provided by the ATO: https://www.ato.gov.au/Calculators-and-tools/Private-health-insurance-rebate-calculator/

If you are not covered by a private hospital insurance policy and you earn above a certain income threshold, you may have to pay the Medicare Levy Surcharge when you lodge your tax return. This only applies after you earn $90,000 for singles or $180,000 for families, however.

How it works is, if you are younger, then the cost of the cover will be lower since the insurers expect you will maintain your cover and you are quite likely healthier and less prone to claim. In recognition of this insurers offer some additional benefits. There are lots of decisions to make here including different levels of cover. It's a bit like a mix 'n' match but not as much fun. I am not able to recommend but for information's sake, check out HBF at https://www.hbf.com.au/

Scroll towards the bottom of the page and there is a wizard which looks just like this, and this tool could help you figure out exactly what sort of cover might be best for you:

Cover to suit your needs

Tell us a little about yourself, and in **3 minutes** we'll find our best cover to suit your needs.

Find my cover

## Life Insurance

In a nutshell,

- it is cheaper when you are younger (less likely to have a claim)

- You will never receive the benefit, but your beneficiaries will

- There are lots of different types, so some learning is involved

- Use a qualified broker to make sure you get what you need

All you could ever want to know with regard to life insurance, and more, can be found at this link here. (Beware, though, it is US based, so some terms may vary. It's just a little information really.) https://www.investopedia.com/terms/l/lifeinsurance.asp#:~:text=%20Types%20of%20Life%20Insurance%20%201%20Term,the%20entire%20premium%20up%20front%20instead...%20More%20

## Income protection insurance

Income protection insurance pays you a benefit if you are unable to work for some time because of illness or injury. This insures you for an agreed level of income and will pay you until you can return to work or for the agreed period – whichever happens first. This is different from redundancy insurance, which offers some financial protection in the case of involuntary redundancy. It is not cheap, but in some circumstances makes sense.

Check out Canstar for a policy that may suit you. Again, this is quite specialised, so a good broker is advised.

## Trauma Insurance

This is a type of cover for traumatic instances like cancer, and pays an agreed amount on diagnosis. Canstar describes it as Trauma insurance cover or critical illness insurance. This provides a lump sum of money to cover immediate medical expenses and other financial needs when a critical illness or injury occurs. Trauma cover pays an agreed amount to cover you for many different issues, such as heart attacks or intensive care.

A serious illness or injury causes more than just physical and emotional turmoil – it has the potential to cause severe disruption to your finances as well. While income protection helps to replace a portion of your income when you cannot work due to illness or injury, it's useful to have a lump sum of money to cover your immediate medical and financial needs. This is where trauma insurance comes into its own. It helps you get on with recovering and getting on with life, without worrying too much about your finances.

## Total & Permanent Disability (TPD)

TPD pays you a cash payout if you become totally and permanently disabled. The definition of total and permanent disability varies quite a bit between insurance companies. It can mean that you are disabled to the extent that you will probably be unable to work again in your occupation or in any job. Not quite sure who defines "probably", though!

Although income protection insurance can help to replace a portion of your income when you are unable to work due to illness or injury, if you are permanently unable to return to work it might also be useful to have a lump sum of money to cover your immediate medical needs as well as to clear any outstanding debts. Total and Permanent Disability (TPD) insurance is used for this purpose.

Since this gets a little tricky, I will just give the link, to guess where? Canstar. https://www.canstar.com.au/life-insurance/tpd-insurance/

## Summary

The insurance salespeople will try to convince you that you need all of the above. You definitely need to consider some life insurance if you have dependants and debt. Beyond that, find out all you can and have a good think about it.

---

### Money Beans Rule 3

---

*If you don't educate yourself, even just a little bit, you are limiting your opportunities.*

# Later Stages in Life

## Kids have gone, finally!

They got the message, they moved! Just kidding. Peace, lower bills, just as much help around the house and food that lasts longer. Now you can enjoy your freedom and have more time to yourself than you could possibly dream of! However, with this newfound freedom, you're suddenly responsible in a different way – you're responsible **only** for yourselves. This is a great time to inspire some soul searching (and finance-working).

Questions to ask are, do you need the larger house? In most cases you don't, so depending on where we are in the real estate cycle perhaps downsizing could be attractive? More often than not it is stressful as heck as the size of the place you are supposed to enjoy might be ridiculously small. Seriously tiny. There is no room for all the things you have amassed over the last 20 – however many years.

We are currently doing that, although the kids are coming with us. What we are doing is shrinking the work – losing the pool, the grass and the upkeep of which that fell on you know who (me, in case you are a bit behind), as well as shrinking some rooms, while retaining space where we need it the most. But for the most part, shrinking is the norm and you will just have to lose the large furniture and adopt a smaller footprint. Not the end of the world, though it may seem like it, at least for a while. Or quite a while. But unless you want to dwell on it, it's time to suck it up and be happy. They are only things.

Blah blah, I hear you say. The point is that generally, downsizing should free up a larger amount of your capital, i.e., money, cash. What to do with this?

It depends on your age, whether you are still working, what you may have in superannuation, just to name the most obvious variables. But if, for example you had borrowed for real estate, or borrowed for shares, then you could consider paying down as much of this debt as you can before investing further. I can't tell you what is best, it simply depends. Again, the Money Beans rules apply (independent advice) so speak to someone who could help you – without bias. That answer tells you nothing really, but do you seriously want another mention of how I cannot advise you?

Ideally, you should enter retirement debt free, owning not only your smaller home, but a decent portfolio of income producing investments, and your super fund. That is true wealth – not necessarily mega millions, but enough to have choices without having to worry about how you will pay for them. If you do have mega millions most likely it is because you followed my wisdom and got started early. Again, you are most welcome!

### *Get a Financial Adviser and Make Sure you Understand Everything.*

There are all sorts of strategies for drawing on your super fund, which cannot be discussed here, but the mix of possibilities, if available to you should lead to an even more financially secure retirement. Given that this may be for 20 or hopefully longer years, it is clearly better that you are comfortable and financially worry free than not! Actually, in an aging population, if you don't get involved in looking out for yourself, the government may not be able to, so then what? If you don't want to believe me, then here is a quote from the Australian Government, (and you have to believe them, even if not me!)

The Australian population is ageing, with older Australians a growing proportion of the total population. In 2017, 15% of Australians (3.8 million) were aged 65 and over; this proportion is projected to grow steadily over the coming decades.

I borrowed their graph to make the point a little stronger. What it means is that more and more of us are getting older and will need looking after. What do you think that means in terms of pensions getting more generous? Not really likely, other than inflation in my view. Probably also the means testing will get tougher so only the truly needy will receive it. If you follow the Money Beans way, you will be part of the self-sufficient group enjoying life and not involved in this level of potential despair.

Figure 1: Proportion of the Australian population aged 65 and over, at 30 June, over time

Per cent

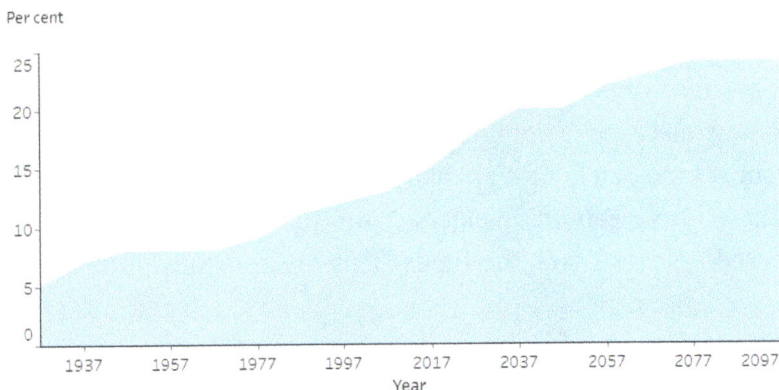

Sources: ABS [1, 2]

## Superannuation Possibilities or what is all this fuss about?

Superguide say that "A good way to begin thinking about your retirement needs and working out a budget is to visit the ASFA Retirement Standard, where you'll find detailed budgets for different households and living standards. The budgets are updated quarterly and assume you own your home. (As a side note try saying ASFA with a mouthful of crisps!)

ASFA suggests singles aged 65 would need around $27,913 a year to live a modest lifestyle while couples need $40,194. A comfortable lifestyle would cost $43,787 for singles and around $61,786 for couples. Some people will be hoping for a retirement lifestyle that is more than comfortable, especially if they are used to a much higher pre-retirement income than $60,000 a year.

To put these figures in perspective, the full Age Pension is currently $24,268 a year for singles and $36,582 for couples. As you can see, this does not stretch to ASFA's modest budget, let alone a comfortable lifestyle, especially for retirees who are paying rent or still paying off a mortgage on top of other expenses.

**See, it's not just my opinion!** Maybe I do have a point? Up to you to decide but I certainly always have an opinion!

The payout stage is tricky with superannuation, and the rules change every now and then. Simply put you can have a pension from your own super fund or a lump sum; and unless there are special hardships and the odd coronavirus pandemic, the funds are what are called preserved. No, not you, the funds. This means hands off until you reach the retirement age.

And then there is the whole interaction with the aged pension. All of this is frankly way too complicated and exceptionally boring. As and when, get some decent financial planning advice and leave the headaches to them. Choose a planner with good recommendations and a whole lot of independence and pay their fees happily. It is worth it, as wrong decisions will cost you, and impinge on your lifestyle which is unacceptable! You can do better than that!

Invest in yourself and get some independent advice.

See Money *Beans Rule 2 and especially 4.*

Please don't be one of those people who get scammed.

# The End

That is it for and from me. I have given you my collected wisdom, bias and opinions. I have shared all I know, (well, much of it) in a light hearted way and if you have made it this far (unless you went to the end right from the start), it means that you might have liked it. I really hope it benefits you, whether you are 18, 45 or 65. Being suddenly responsible can be a little daunting. This book has much of what you need to be undaunted. Yes, I know there is probably no such word. Oh, there is. How about that?

You now have the tools. Challenge everything, seek other opinions and educate yourself. Follow people who seem honest and seek unbiased advice. Keep it simple, keep saving, and you will have more than enough wealth to have the choices that make life even more wonderful.

Perhaps your next phase is suddenly wealthy? I sincerely hope so.

All the very best

David Bay

# Gems amongst the Sharks

Over the years I have discovered a few gems out there. I am not paid, nor will be paid by listing any of them, but since you have invested in my book, you get these gems, my ideas and views, and biases, as a bonus! (That is in addition to the humour and almost total disrespect of many others).

Some of my favourite things, (no it's not the Sound of Music, well maybe it is). They are not recommendations; you must do your own research; they are purely businesses that I have used and continue to use.

1. BellDirect or CMC – these are both low brokerage websites that are easy to use and offer fantastic service and research. Commsec is also popular and a good platform. I use it for my smurf.

2. Macquarie Bank for at least their cash management trust. Comes with apps and all of that (because how can you be proper without an app?) and they are very professional to deal with. It would not hurt to build a relationship with them.

3. The Trading Game – this is a paid course run by Louise Bedford and Chris Tate. The course is not cheap, but the quality is unsurpassed. They have other great material including books on charting which you will find here. https://www.tradinggame.com.au/product-shop/specials/

4. The Motley Fool. They have an abundance of free material and also paid subscriptions. I suggest that you read them for a while and see if you like their style. You might then consider a paid service. It's like having a team of analysts on your side.

5. Marcus Today. They have a fantastic newsletter and offer other paid services as well. I have only discovered this team lately, and am so far very impressed, and given I am cynical, this is high praise indeed. They offer a free trial to the newsletter so nothing to lose. Straight advice, probably not for the beginner with a take it or leave it style; that is my style, and they do it well. Free e-books are here https://marcustoday.com.au/ebook/ and a free trial is here https://marcustoday.com.au/trial-sign-up/.

6. Try the smaller banks for service and friendliness. I think most of the majors are all much the same for transactional banking. There are differences when it comes to loans, and that is why my last recommendation is me to help you choose.

   CUA Bank is friendly https://ob.cua.com.au/ .

7. ASX website has a lot of learning material. Try https://www.asx.com.au/education/shares-course.htm

8. David Bay – Liberty Adviser – mortgage broker with access to a wide range of loans with great advice. All round nice guy and now published author. – See, humour to the end. If you are in Australia, happy to try and help. If not, then consider moving here. I can wait. Big surprise since compliance lurks everywhere; if you take a loan through me, I will earn fees. Who would have thought?

# Beginners Education Glossary

This glossary has been gratefully copied with kind permission from the **Marcus Today** website

https://marcustoday.com.au/2019/08/beginners-education-glossary-a-h/

**Thanks to Marcus Padley and team.**

## A

**Australian Clearing House – ACH** – The Australian Clearing House Pty Ltd, the subsidiary of ASX which clears options and futures traded on the ASX.

**Australian Financial Services Licence** – A licence granted by ASIC that authorises a person who carries on a financial services business to provide financial services.

**Accumulation fund** – A superannuation fund where benefits received by members include investment earning plus employer contributions. (As opposed to a defined contribution or defined benefit fund).

**Accumulation index** – Index measuring movements in the markets value. It takes account of both price movement and income (dividend) growth & assumes income is reinvested.

**Accrual accounting** – Revenues and expenses are recorded as they are earned, regardless of whether cash has been paid or received.

**ADR – American Depository Receipt** – Certificates that represent a non-U.S. company's publicly traded equity or debt. They trade in USD on an American exchange or over-the-counter market.

**AGM – Annual General Meeting** – Annual meeting between company directors and shareholders. The meeting covers company performance and outlook, and shareholders vote on key issues relating to the company.

**All Ordinaries Index (XAO)** – The predominant measure of overall Australian sharemarket performance. Made up of weighted average share prices Australia's 500 largest listed companies, approximately. Established at 500 points at January 1980. More recently called the S&P/All                                    Ordinaries.

**All Ordinaries Accumulation Index (XAOAI)** – Takes into account both capital appreciation and dividends as a return on the companies in the All Ordinaries index.

**Annual report** – Company document issued after the end of a company's financial year, describing company's annual activities and performance. It includes a profit and loss statement, balance sheet and a statement of cash flows.

**Annual Yield** – Annual yield represents the dividend return from an investment. It is calculated by dividing the dividend per share by the current market share price, converted to a percentage. **ASIC – Australian Securities and Investments Commission** – The Federal Government authority responsible for administering companies and securities law.

**Asset allocation** – The process of choosing between assets classes or individual company assets when constructing a portfolio.

**Asset backing** – The value of a company›s assets divided by the number of shares on issue. Can be related to a firm's earnings capacity.

**ASX – Australian Stock Exchange**– Australia's national stock exchange for trading equities, government bonds and other fixed interest securities.

**ASX 200 (AXJO)** – Similar to the All Ordinaries Index but made up on only the 200 largest listed companies.

**At the market** – A term used to describe an order to buy or sell a stock at the best price obtainable at the time.

**At the money** – Term used to describe an option or a warrant with an exercise price equal to the current market price of the underlying asset.

**Alpha** – The expected return of a stock or a portfolio if the market rate of return is zero.

**American option** – An option that can be exercised before and up to its expiration date.

**Amortisation** – The accounting process where an interest-bearing liability such as a mortgage is paid off over time through regular instalments that comprise both principal and interest.

**Annualise** – The process of converting the rate of return on an investment for periods other than a full year to annual terms.

**Annuity** – A financial arrangement in which periodic payments are made to the annuity holder in exchange for the investment of a lump sum amount.

**Appreciation** – Refers to an increase in the value of an asset.

**Arbitrage** – The process of buying an asset at a price in one market, and sell it at a higher price in another market, taking advantage of current prices in different markets.

**Ask price** – The price at which a holder of an asset is willing to sell that asset (opposite of bid).

**Authorised Capital** – The amount of share capital which a company is permitted to issue. Also called nominal capital.

**B**

**Balance sheet** – A financial statement that reveals a company's assets, liabilities and shareholders' equity at a point in time.

**Balanced fund** – A superannuation fund that diversifies its holdings over a range of asset classes such as shares, bonds, property and cash.

**Basis** – The price difference between the spot price of an asset and the price for the derivatives relating to that asset.

**Basis point** – One percent of one percent (0.01%)

**Basis risk** – The risk linked to uncertain movements in the spread between a futures price and a spot price. The amount the value of a derivative differs from the value of the asset underlying it.

**Bearish** – A view that markets will fall.

**Bear market** – A pessimistic market characterised by falling prices (opposite of bullish market).

**Below par** – A price below the face/par value of a security.

**Benchmark** – A yardstick used to compare performance of securities.

**Beta** – A measure of how historical changes in a share price have correlated to overall movements in the share market as a whole. Market beta is 1.0. Shares with beta > 1 are more reactive, those with <1 are less reactive to market movements.

**Bid price** – The price that a prospective buyer is willing to pay for an asset (opposite of ask).

**Bid-ask spread** – The difference between the bid and ask price for a security.

**Block trade** – Off-market trading mechanism enabling market users to transact orders of significant size in specified contracts.

**Blue chip** – Refers to shares in leading companies that have a reputation for excellent quality and sound financial management.

**Bond** – A security that obligates the borrower to make specified payments (coupons) to the bondholder over the life of the bond, and repays the face value at maturity.

**Books close date** – The date at which a company's share register is closed off to identify the shareholders and to calculate any entitlement to new issues and dividends.

**Book value** – An accounting measure that gives the net worth of an asset according to its carrying value on the company's balance sheet.

**Breakout** – When a market has been trading within consolidation then moves outside this range. The price is then expected to continue moving in the direction of the break.

**Brent crude** – A major benchmark of oil worldwide.

**Broker** – The intermediary who acts as the go-between in security transactions.

**Brokerage** – The fee charged by a broker for processing a securities transaction.

**Bullish** – Belief that prices in markets are going to rise.

**Bull Market** – A prolonged period of rising security prices.

**C**

**Call option** – An option that gives the holder the right but not the obligation to purchase an asset for a pre-determined price (the exercise price) at or before its expiration date.

**Capital gain** – The amount by which the sale price of an asset exceeds its purchase price.

**Capital loss** – The loss, which may be offset against current or future capital gains, that an investor makes on a transaction.

**Capital growth** – The appreciation of the market value of an asset.

**Capitalisation or Market Capitalisation** – A company's share price multiplied by the total number of shares issued by that company.

**Cash rate – Interbank overnight rate –** The interest rate which banks charge to lend funds to other banks on an overnight unsecured basis. The RBA calculates and publishes this cash rate each day on the basis of data collected directly from banks.

**Cash rate target –** A target for the cash rate or overnight interest rate. A tool in monetary policy specified by the Reserve Bank of Australia.

**CGT – Capital gains tax –** Tax imposed on the profit arising from the sale of a capital asset such shares or property.

**Charting –** An aspect of technical analysis using share price charts to make buy and sell decisions.

**CHESS – Clearing House Electronic Subregister System –** The system that allows the automatic transfer and settlement of ASX transactions via computer processing. Replaces old share certificates system.

**Churning –** The process of acquiring a share holding in a company, and then placing buy and sell orders for shares of that company in order to build up turnover.

**Client adviser –** The individual who provides you with advice at a full-service broker.

**Closed end fund –** A fund whose shares are traded through a stock exchange. Shares can only be redeemed at their market value, not at their net asset value.

**Commission –** See brokerage.

**Concise financial report –** A summarised version of the annual report provided to shareholders if a full annual report is not requested.

**Contract note –** A written document confirming a transaction between a broker and a client which describes the costs, type and quantity of shares traded. Also known as a ‹Confirmation›.

**Cumulative** – The right of some preference shares to receive a dividend even though none has been declared. Payments become an arrear.

**Commodity** – The term covers a wide range of items that can be traded, including metals and agricultural goods.

**Common stock** – Equities issued as ownership shares in a publicly listed company. They entitle the holder to voting rights and a share of the dividend payments periodically announced by the company.

**Compound interest** – A form of interest calculation, where in each period interest is calculated on both the principal and the interest previously accrued.

**Consolidation** – A period where the market trades in a broad sideways pattern within a trend. Consolidations usually follow a strong market gain or fall. It will end with the market resuming its trend or if the market heads in the opposite direction having formed a top or bottom.

**Credit risk** – The risk that counterparty to a financial obligation such as a loan will default on repayments linked to the obligation.

**Cum dividend** – Shares quoted cum dividend entitle the buyer to the current dividend. The price of the shares will usually reflect the amount of the dividend.

**Currency risk** – The risk that an investor will incur losses on an overseas investment as a result of adverse shifts in exchange rates.

**Current ratio** – The ratio of a company's current assets to current liabilities A measure of liquidity that shows a company's ability to pay off its current liabilities by liquidating its current assets.

# D

**Daily settlement price** – The official daily quotation for each Contract available on a Market of the Exchange for each delivery or cash settlement month as determined by the Exchange for the purpose of margining by the Clearing House.

**Day orders** – Orders which automatically expire at the close of the day's trading if not filled during the day they are received.

**DCF – Discounted Cash-Flow** – A valuation method that accounts for differences in the timing of cash flows, by discounting these cash flows to their present values.

**Debt to equity ratio** – Shows the relationship between funds provided by borrowing and funds provided by shareholders. The debt/equity ratio shows to what extent a company is financed by debt (also called the gearing or leverage ratio)

**Delisting** – Is when a company's shares are removed from the Official list. Reasons for removal include a company failing to comply with the exchange's rules or no longer meeting listing requirements.

**Delivery** – The actual transfer of possession of securities from one counterparty to another.

**Demutualisation** – The process of changing from a company owned by members to a (not necessarily publicly owned) company owned by shareholders.

**Depreciation** – The gradual writing down of the cost of an asset over the useful life of that asset.

**Depression** – A period during which business activity drops significantly. High unemployment rates and deflation often accompany a depression.

**Derivatives** – These are a class of securities, including futures and options, which derive their value from underlying physical securities.

**Director** – A member of a company's board who is charged with overseeing the affairs of the company, and ensuring that senior management acts in shareholders' interests.

**Discount** – The amount by which the current value of a share is below its asset backing.

**Discounting** – The term used to describe the procedure of calculating the present value of a stream of future cash flows.

**Discretionary account** – The account of a customer who gives the broker the authority to make buy and sell decisions on the customer's behalf.

**Distribution** – Income emanating from a trust, similar to a dividend from a company.

**Divergence** – When the RSI or MACD indicators broadly move in the opposite direction to that of the actual market price. Divergence can be positive or negative.

**Diversification** – Spreading a portfolio over a number of investments in order to limit exposure to any one form of risk.

**Dividend** – Distribution of part of the company's net profit paid out to shareholders, expressed as a number of cents per share. To receive a declared dividend the shares must be purchased before the ex-dividend date.

**Dividend imputation** – An Australian tax rule where the amount of corporate tax paid by a company is credited to shareholders of that company. The shareholder is assessed on the sum of the total amount of dividend and the imputation credit, but is allowed to claim the imputation credit as a tax rebate.

**Dividend payout ratio** – The percentage of earnings paid out as dividends.

**Dividend type** – Dividends will be classified as either interim, final or special. The last dividend in the financial year is final, other regular dividends are interim, and special dividends are those not paid regularly each year.

**Dividend yield** – A rate of return measure, calculated by dividing the annual dividend per share by the current market price of the share.

**Dow Jones** – The Dow Jones Industrial Average is the average of 30 large blue chip US corporations. It has been computed since 1896, a history that has aided its broad recognition across the world.

**DPS – Dividends per share** – The amount of earnings paid out to shareholders on a per share basis adjusted by a dilution factor to take account of issues and reconstructions.

**DRP – Distribution Reinvestment Plan** – An alternative to cash dividends, allowing shareholders to receive new shares instead of cash. These shares are often issued at a discount and no brokerage is paid.

**Due diligence** – The process of checking the accuracy of information contained in a company public statement, such as a prospectus, before recommending that company to others. Is also the act of one company investigating another company before buying its shares.

**E**

**Earnings retention ratio** – The percentage of earnings retained by a company (i.e., that portion of earnings not paid out in dividends).

**Earnings yield** – The ratio of earnings per share to the price of that share (the reciprocal of the price-earnings ratio).

**EBIT – Earnings before interest & taxes** – A key earnings measure.

Similar to net profit, except that the effects of tax benefits, deductions and loans are factored out, providing a better measure of company's underlying performance.

**EBITDA – Earnings before interest, taxes, depreciation and amortization.**

**Electronic holding statement** – Evidence of your securities ownership in the form of a holding statement. All security holdings on ASX are registered electronically.

**EPS – earnings per share** – Measures the earnings that are attributed to each equivalent ordinary share over a twelve-month period. It is calculated by dividing the company's earnings by the number of shares on issue

**Equities** – Synonym for shares and represents part-ownership of a company, as distinct from debt securities such as bonds and debentures.

**Equity** – Another word for a share investment. It can also mean the value an owner has in any asset after debt on that investment is deducted.

**Escrow** – A financial arrangement where two parties utilise a third party to temporarily hold money or assets for a transaction on their behalf, until the time the transaction is complete.

**Eurodollars** – US dollar-denominated deposits at non-US banks or foreign branches of US banks.

**Euromarkets** – A generic term referring to international markets for currencies outside of each currency's home marketplace.

**European option** – An option that can only be exercised on its expiration date.

**Exchange rate** – The price of one unit of a particular country's currency in terms of another country's currency.

**Ex-date** – Date on which shares change from being quoted "cum" to "ex". It is usually the fourth business day prior to the record date.

**Ex-dividend** – Shares sold ex-dividend entitle the seller to retain the current dividend. Shares are usually quoted ex-dividend five business days before the company's books close.

**Ex-dividend date** – Four business days before the company's Record Date. To be entitled to a dividend a shareholder must have purchased shares before the ex-dividend date.

**Execution only broker** – A broker who processes the transaction but is not permitted to provide advice on securities transactions. Sometimes known as a 'discount' broker.

**F**

**Face value** – The amount repaid on a bond or income security at maturity and the amount on which distributions are calculated.

**Fed** – Short for the US Federal Reserve, the US central bank.

**Financial year** – The period over which a company measures its performance. The most common financial year ends on 30 June every year.

**Fixed interest asset** – A security such as a Treasury bond that pays a specified cashflow over a specified period and pays back the face value of the security at maturity.

**Fixed interest** – A type of debt that pays a fixed annual rate of interest.

**Float** – A new issue of shares in a company before it lists on the stock exchange. Also known as an IPO.

**Flight to quality** – The process where investors seek out less risky investments in times of economic uncertainty.

**Floating rate bond** – A bond whose interest rate is reset periodically relative to a specified market rate.

**FOMC – Federal Open Market Committee** – Part of the US Federal Reserve. Determines interest policy in the US.

**Franking Credit** – Used in a dividend imputation system and represent the portion of a dividend to which a company has already paid taxation. Shareholders then include the grossed-up amount of the dividend (pre-tax) and then have their income tax payable calculated using that grossed up dividend. Franking credits are then used to offset tax payable.

**Franked Dividend** – Dividend paid by a company out of profits on which the company has already paid tax.

The investor is entitled to an imputation credit, or reduction in the amount of income tax that must be paid, up to the amount of tax already paid by the company.

**Franking** – The percentage of the dividend on which the company has already paid tax.

**FTSE – Financial Times Stock Exchange** – The UK equivalent of Australia's S&P/All Ordinaries share price index, it is a value-weighted index of 100 of the largest companies listed on the London Stock Exchange.

**Full-service broker** – A broker who provides you with advice on securities transactions, and other services such as research and access to floats.

**Fully diluted earnings per share** – Earnings per share of a stock after converting all options, warrants and convertible securities into equivalent common stock.

**Fundamental Analysis** – Method of analysis using ratios and percentages calculated from financial data of a company to assess the company's quantitative and qualitative aspects.

**Fundamentals** – A company's financial and operational details. Fundamental analysts assess these factors in an attempt to determine the long-term performance of the business, and ultimately, the company's share price performance.

**Fund manager** – A professional who buys and sells investments for a managed fund.

**Futures** – Futures are contracts to buy or sell a particular asset (or cash equivalent) on a specified future date at a price agreed today.

**G**

**GDP – Gross Domestic Product** – The total value of all goods and services produced within a country in a given time period (usually a year or quarter).

**Gearing** – Process of increasing funds available for investment through borrowing. The ratio of debt finance to equity finance or, as the use of long-term debt in financing an entity. Gearing may be measured as EBIT/EBIT-Interest.

**H**

**Hang Seng index** – The main Hong Kong share price index, similar to Australia›s S&P/All Ordinaries index.

**Hedge** – Transaction which reduces or offsets the risk of a current holding, involves the purchase of an offsetting position to guard against the risk of a market decline.

**Hedge fund** – A higher risk managed fund. Fund managers funds have greater scope to use derivatives, short positions, and exotic securities to boost returns using aggressive and specialized strategies.

**Historical Yield** – The yield on an investment based on the end of period price, but using distributions or dividends previously paid over the relevant period.

**Holding period return** – The rate of return over a given period.

**Holding statement** – The document which notifies you of your shareholding in a particular company.

# I

**Imputation credit** – Tax credits passed on to a shareholder who receives a franked dividend.

Imputation credits entitle investors to a rebate for tax already paid by an Australian company

**Indicators** – Analytical tools used by technical analysts to help them select shares.

**Inflation** – The increase in the prices paid for goods and services, measured by the Consumer Price Index.

**Institutional Investor** – An organisation with large investable funds whose primary purpose is to invest its own assets or those held in trust for others.

**Interbank overnight rate** – See 'Cash rate'

**Intrinsic value** – The underlying worth of a business, calculated by analysing a company's fundamentals.
**IMF – International monetary fund** – An organisation of 185 member countries. Among other aims it was established to promote international monetary co-operation, and provide temporary financial assistance to countries.

**Implied volatility** – The standard deviation of stock returns that is consistent with an option's market value.

**Index** – Is a means of measuring returns from and performance of a portfolio of selected investments. The S&P/ASX200 Index acts as a proxy for the overall performance of the larger vehicles in the market or sector.

**Indexing** – A passive portfolio management strategy that seeks to match the composition, and therefore the performance, of a selected market index.

**In the money** – This describes an option that would generate profits if exercised now – when the exercise price of a call (put) option or warrant is below (above) the current market price of the underlying asset.

**Income statement** – A financial statement that exhibits a company's revenues and expenses (or profit/loss position) over a specified period.

**Index fund** – A fund that holds shares in proportion to their representation in a broad market index such as the S&P/All Ordinaries index.

**Inflation** – A measure of the change in the general level of prices. A proxy is generally taken to be the change in the consumer price index.

**Inflation target** – The preferred range for the rate of inflation used a guidance tool for monetary policy. Australia's inflation target is between 2%-3%.

**Insider trading** – An illegal activity that involves trading based on information that is not yet publicly available to the markets.

**Interest coverage ratio** – A measure of a company's leverage. It equals EBIT divided by interest expense and provides an indication of a company's ability to meet interest payments. The higher the interest cover, the greater the company's ability to meet interest payments.

**Interest rate swaps** – Where two parties trade the cashflows corresponding to different securities without actually exchanging ownership on those securities.

**Institutional Placement** – When a company raises capital through placing stock with institutional investors who are willing to take the price on offer.

**IPO – Initial Public Offering** – Initial capital raising by public subscription to securities, such as shares offered on the share market for the first time. Also known as a Float.

**IRR – Internal Rate of Return** – The discount rate at which the net present value of an investment is equal to zero. The total rate of return generated by an investment over its life or a given timescale, taking into account sale and purchase prices and all cash flows associated with the holding.

**Issued capital** – The value of securities allotted in a company to its shareholders and debt holders.

# L

**Leverage** – See gearing.

**Leverage ratio** – A ratio of a company's debt to that same company's shareholders' equity.

**Limited liability company** – A company where shareholders have no personal liability to the creditors of that company should it go bankrupt.

**Liquidity** – This term relates to the speed at which an asset can be converted to cash.

**LIBOR – London Interbank Offered Rate** – The rate at which creditworthy banks charge each other for large loans of Eurodollars in the London market.

**LME – London Metals Exchange** – The primary exchange for the global trade of base metals and other related commodities.

**Long position** – Where an investor has an excess of purchases over sales of a particular asset at a point in time.

**Long term** – An investment period that usually refers to a time period of several years or longer.

**M**

**Macroeconomics** – That area of economics that focuses on analysis of broad trends in a country's economy. Key components of macroeconomics are monetary policy and fiscal policy.

**Market capitalization** – See capitalization.

**Maintenance margin** – A value below which a trader's margin must not fall. If the margin falls below the maintenance margin, a margin call occurs.

**Managed fund** – A trust where you pool your resources with other investors, and which is run by a professional fund manager.

**Margin** – A deposit lodged with an exchange or clearing house to cover the risk of financial loss due to adverse movements in market prices. May also describe financial assets, like stocks, that are purchased through money borrowed by a broker.

**Margin call** – A requirement by a clearinghouse that a clearing member increases margin deposits to cover for an adverse shift in prices on futures contracts held on its books.

**Margin lending** – A type of borrowing to buy shares which requires you to maintain the lender's proportion of your portfolio value above an agreed level. If the portfolio value falls, the lender will issue you with a margin call, which requires you to provide securities or cash to maintain the lender's proportion.

**Market timing** – Asset allocation where investments in particular markets are increased when the investor expects that market to outperform other markets or the overall market.

**Market-book ratio** – The market price of a share divided by the book value per share.

**Market value** – The current value of a security.

**Marking to market** – Pricing an asset at today's market value, and not at the book value of that asset. Can also describe the daily settlement of obligations on futures positions.

**Market portfolio** – The portfolio for which each security is held in proportion to its market value.

**Market risk** – Sometimes called systemic risk. The risk of a general decline in the market, attributable to macroeconomic factors.

**Market timer** – An investor who speculates on broad market moves, rather than on individual securities.

**Merger** – A form of corporate restructure in which two companies merge their businesses. Unlike takeovers, mergers are usually a result of a mutually beneficial negotiation process.

**Mean Reversion** – The notion that asset values revert to an average value or to an equilibrium value.

**MER – Management Expense Ratio** – The amount of fees charged by the Manager divided by the total assets of the trust. This generally includes all ongoing fees. Such as fund management fees, trustee fees and custody fees.

**MACD – Moving Average Convergence Divergence** – An indicator that follows the difference between a series of moving averages. Buy and sell signals are generated when the MACD line rises above or below the signal line. It has the ability capture wide swinging moves in markets.

**Microeconomics** – The branch of economics that studies the decision making and interactions of individuals and firms.

**N**

**NAB – Net Asset Backing** – Net assets divided by the number of securities on issue.

**Nasdaq** – An American stock exchange and **the** second largest exchange in the world (by market cap).

**Nasdaq Composite Index** – An index of all stocks traded on the electronic Nasdaq exchange. Typically

**NAV -Net Asset Value** – Total assets minus total liabilities.

**Negative gearing** – Borrowing money to acquire assets where the interest payments exceed income from the assets, which generates a tax deduction.

**Net assets** – Total assets less total liabilities for a company at a point in time.

**Nikkei Index** – A bellwether Japanese share price index that covers the top 225 shares listed on the Tokyo Stock Exchange.

**Nominal interest rate** – The interest rate in terms of nominal dollars.

**Non-Renounceable rights** – The holder of the rights does not have the ability to sell on the ASX.

**Nonsystematic risk** – Firm-specific risk factors.

**NPAT– Net Profit after Tax** – The profit a company is left with from operating its business.

**NTA** – Total assets minus intangible assets such as goodwill.

# O

**Official List** – The list of companies that trade on the ASX, as maintained by the exchange itself.

**OECD – Organisation for Economic Co-operation and Development**

Represents 30 countries with a commitment to a market economy. Among other aims, it seeks to encourage economic growth and financial stability among member countries.

**Offer** – The price at which a holder is prepared to sell an asset (similar to ask).

**Open interest** – The number of futures contracts outstanding.

**Option** – A contract between two parties, which gives the holder, the right, but not the obligation, to buy or sell the asset underlying the option at a pre-determined price (the exercise price) on or prior to a particular time in the future (the expiration date).

**Ordinary shares** – Holders of ordinary shares are part-owners of a company and may receive payments in cash, called dividends, if the company trades profitably. A class of shares which have no preferential rights as to either dividends out of profits or capital on a winding up.

**Out of the money** – Describes an option that would not be profitable if exercised now (the opposite of in the money)

**Over-the-counter market** – In informal group of dealers and/or brokers who trade in a market. However, there is not a formal exchange.

**P**

**Passive management** – The creation of a well-diversified portfolio that replicates a broad-based market index such as the S&P/All Ordinaries share price index.

**Pcp** – Previous corresponding period.

**PER or P/E – Price-earnings ratio** – Measures the current price of a share divided by its annual current or forecast earnings of that same share. Commonly used to measure the attractiveness of particular shares compared to other companies or to the industry. Growth stocks tend to have a high P/E ratios compared to income stocks.

**Placement** – An off-market issue of units to sophisticated investors generally institutions.

**Portfolio** – A collection of different investments held by an investor.

**Preference share** – Shares that take priority over a company's ordinary shares for dividends and any distribution in the event of liquidation. Dividends are usually referenced to a fixed or floating interest rate and can be franked or unfranked.

**Privatisation** – The alteration of the legal and managerial structure of a government body to permit private equity holdings or outright ownership. This occurred when companies Telstra, Qantas and Commonwealth Bank were listed.

**Portfolio Turnover (Velocity)** – A measure of the trading activity in a fund's portfolio of investments — that is, how often securities are bought and sold by the fund. Also known as velocity.

**Premium** – The purchase price of an option.

**Present value** – The present day value of a future amount, determined by discounting this future amount by an appropriate discount rate.

**Price / Operating Cash Flow ratio** – This ratio compares a company's share price with the cash flow per share. We use two Price/OCF ratios, one including Capital Expenditure, and one before (or excluding) Capital Expenditure.

**Primary market** – The market into which shares are sold when they are first issued.

**Product Disclosure Statement** – A PDS is the offer document that contains information inviting investment in the securities of an ASIC-registered investment scheme. A PDS generally contains financial and other information about the company and its operations as well as risk and risk mitigating strategies.

**Profit and Loss Account (P&L Account)** – A major financial statement showing a company's earnings and expenses over a given period of time.

**Prospectus** – A statement approved by ASIC that provides details of an upcoming securities issue to the public.

**Private placement** – An issue of bonds or stocks that are sold directly to a select group of (often institutional) investors.

**Proxy** – This allows an agent to vote on an issue relating to a company in the name of a shareholder in that company.

**Public offering** – An issue of bonds or stocks to the entire market.

**Pullback** – After a strong trend the market retraces a small portion of that move before resuming its trend. This differs from a consolidation, which trades sideways. Pullbacks are usually short and small in magnitude (typically less than 30% of the rise).

**Put option** – The right but not the obligation to sell an asset at a specified exercise price on or before a specified expiration date.

**R**

**RBA – Reserve Bank of Australia** – Australia's central bank. The controller of monetary policy in Australia.

**Redeemable preference share** – Preference shares that can be redeemed for a fixed amount of cash or shares.

**Recession** – A decline in GDP for two or more consecutive quarters.

**Record Date** – Date used in determining who is entitled to a dividend. Those on the register at the record are eligible for the entitlement.

**Return** – The percentage an investment has earned or might earn.

**Real interest rate** – The excess of the nominal interest rate less the inflation rate.

**REIT – Real Estate Investment Trust** – A global term for a corporation or trust that pools the capital of investors to purchase and manage income generating property (equity REIT) and/or mortgage loans (mortgage REIT). REITs are traded on major exchanges just like stocks. They are also granted special tax considerations.

**Relative Strength Indicator (RSI)** – An indicator used to measure the underlying strength of a market move. It attempts to anticipate a change in trend when it crosses above or below upper and lower limits which suggests that a stock has become overbought or oversold.

**Renounceable rights** – The holder of the rights has the ability to sell on the ASX.

**Responsible Entity – RE** – A public company holding an Australian Financial Services Licence who has been authorised by the Australian Securities & Investments Commission to operate a registered managed investments scheme.

**Resistance level** – This is a term often used in technical analysis. It describes a price level above which it is supposedly difficult for a stock to rise above.

**ROA – Return on assets** – An earnings measure that is earnings after tax divided by total assets.

**ROE – Return on equity** – An earnings measure that is earnings after tax divided by shareholders' equity.

**Rights issue** – An offer made to existing shareholders in a company to buy new shares to be issued by that company at a discount to the prevailing market price.

**Risk** – The recognition that outcomes are uncertain. For more detail see credit risk, currency risk, interest rate risk and systematic risk.

**Risk-free asset** – In theory such an asset does not exist, although the market use gilt edged government debt such as Australian Treasury notes as a proxy for a risk-free asset.

**Risk-free rate** – An interest rate that can be earned with certainty.

**Risk premium** – The expected return in excess of that on risk-free asset. The premium compensates the investor for taking on the riskier investment.

**S**

**S&P 500** – An index made up of the 500 largest companies listed on American stock exchanges.

**Security** – General term for the instruments that signify ownership of an asset class. Units, shares or bonds are all types of 'security'.

**Settlement date** – The date, three days after the transaction, by which you must supply cash or documentation for a securities purchase or sale.

**Shares or stocks** – Shares represent part-ownership in a company. They can be ordinary shares, preference shares or partly-paid (contributing) shares.

**Share registry** – An organisation which, on behalf of a company, records changes in share ownership, issues shareholding statements, and makes adjustments for dividend payments, bonus and rights issues.

**Short term** – An investment period that usually refers to days or months rather than years.

**SEATS – Stock Exchange Automated Trading System** – This is a computer network that allows stockbrokers to trade via computer terminals.

**Secondary market** – The market where securities already in existence are bought and sold (can be on an exchange or over-the-counter market).

**Securities** – A financial instrument, which is a claim over an asset or a future income stream. Examples are bonds and shares.

**Securitisation** – The pooling together of similar loans into standardised bonds. These bonds use the interest paid on the underlying loans to pay interest to the bondholders.

**SPP – Share Purchase Plan** – Typically accompanies an institutional placement and allows retail investors to take part in a company's capital raising.

**Short position** – Where an investor has an excess of sales over purchases of a particular asset at a point in time.

**Shorting a market** – A strategy where the investor sells an asset that she does not own. It entails the investor borrowing the asset from a broker, and then giving it back to the broker when the loan is repaid.

**Speculation** – The purchase of a risky investment in anticipation of greater returns.

**Spot rate (or spot price)** – The current interest rate (or price) on offer for an asset.

**Spread** – The difference between the current bid and the current ask (in over-the-counter trading) or offered (in exchange trading) of a given security

**Standard deviation** – A statistic that measures dispersion around a particular point.

**Stapled Security** – When the unitholder owns a unit in the Trust and a unit in the attached Company, which cannot be separately traded.

**Statement of cash flows** – A financial statement that shows a company's cash receipts and cash payments over a specified period, such as a year.

**Stock exchange** – A secondary market where already issued securities are bought and sold such as the Australian Stock Exchange (ASX).

**Stock split** – Where a company issues new shares in exchange for the shares it currently has on issue. These splits can result in fewer shares on issue, or more shares on issue.

**Stop-loss order** – A sell order to be made if the price of a stock holding falls below a pre specified level.

**Support level** – This is a term often used in technical analysis. It describes a price level below which it is supposedly difficult for a stock to fall.

**Systematic risk** – Similar in meaning to market risk. It refers to risk attributable to macroeconomic factors

**T**

**Target or Price Target** – Usually refers to a brokers expected share price in 12 months-time.

**Technical analysis** – Method used to selecting shares through the study of price action. Charts representing past price movements and volume, are the principle tools used to identify trends on which future predictions are made.

**TED spread** – An indicator of perceived credit risk in the general economy. The difference between the three-month T-bill interest rate and three-month LIBOR. T-bills are considered risk-free while LIBOR reflects the credit risk of lending to commercial banks.

**Tracking Error** – The difference between the returns achieved on an index-based portfolio of assets and the performance achieved by the index it follows. Tracking error measures the standard deviation of the excess returns of a portfolio of securities compared to its benchmark.

**Treasury bonds** – A bond issued by the Australian Government to assist in its financing requirements. They can have maturities out to 15 years.

**Treasury notes** – A shorter-term security issued by the Australian Government. They can have maturities of 5, 13 or 26 weeks, and are generally used for liquidity management purposes.

**Trust** – A type of investment structure where investors hold their interest in units rather than shares.

**Trustee** – One who beneficially holds property on behalf of another under a trust.

**Turnover (velocity)** – The number of units in a particular stock traded on the ASX over a period of time.

# U

**Underwriter** – Underwriters purchase shares or bonds from the issuing company and resell them, receiving a fee for this service. They agree to purchase any unsold shares in an issue of shares.

**Unitholder** – The person registered under the provisions of the Trust Deed as the holder of a unit in the Trust. Includes persons jointly registered.

**Unit Trust** – A collective fund which holds a portfolio of securities on behalf of the investors who hold units in the trust.

# V

**Valuation** – A value for a business that is derived by fundamental analysis.

**VIX Volatility Index** – The Chicago Board of Trade's volatility index, measures the cost of using options as insurance against declines in the S&P 500.

**Volatility** – Measure of the amount of fluctuation in price of the underlying asset calculated using the standard deviation of average daily price change.

**VWAP** – Volume weighted average price.

# W

**WACC** – Weighted average cost of capital.

**Warrants** – Financial instruments issued by banks, governments and products with investment purposes and those for trading purposes; warrants may be issued over securities (such as shares), a basket of securities, a share price index, currencies or commodities **Working Capital** – Current assets less current liabilities. A measure of the long-term investment required to finance the day-to-day operations at a given.

**WTI – West Texas Intermediate** – The benchmark price of oil.

**Y**

**Yield** – The total dividends received over the previous 12-month period expressed as a percentage of the current share price.

# References

(Sources where information was *"borrowed"* from, ☺

Endnotes

I.      Finder. Credit Card Statistics https://www.finder.com.au/credit-cards/credit-card-statistics

II.     Moneysmart Compound Interest Calculator. https://moneysmart.gov.au/budgeting/compound-interest-calculator?

III.    Canstar Transaction Accounts. https://www.canstar.com.au/transaction-accounts/

IV.     Money Smart – How Super Works. https://moneysmart.gov.au/how-super-works/choosing-a-super-fund

V.      Superguide https://www.superguide.com.au/boost-your-superannuation/comparing-super-funds-check-out-the-cheapest-funds

VI.     Australian Taxation Office. Deductions you can claim. https://www.ato.gov.au/individuals/income-and-deductions/deductions-you-can-claim/

VII.    Australian Institute of Health and Welfare. Australian Government. https://www.aihw.gov.au/reports/life-expectancy-death/deaths-in-australia/contents/life-expectancy

VIII.   Wikipedia https://en.wikipedia.org/wiki/List_of_countries_by_home_ownership_rate

IX.     Australian Taxation Office https://www.ato.gov.au/Individuals/Investing/

X.      Investopedia https://www.investopedia.com/ask/answers/what-stock-split-why-do-stocks-split/

XI.     Canstar https://www.canstar.com.au/home-loans/

XII.    Australian Bureau of Statistics. https://www.abs.gov.au/ausstats/abs@.nsf/Lookup/by%20Subject/4130.0~2017-18~Media%20Release~More%20households%20renting%20as%20home%20ownership%20falls%20(Media%20Release)~10

XIII.  Reserve Bank of Australia. https://www.rba.gov.au/media-releases/2020/mr-20-01.html

XIV.  Trading Economics. https://tradingeconomics.com/australia/interest-rate#:~:text=Interest%20Rate%20in%20Australia%20averaged,percent%20in%20March%20of%202020.

XV.  Private Health. Australian Government. https://www.privatehealth.gov.au/health_insurance/surcharges_incentives/insurance_rebate.htm

XVI.  Canstar        https://www.canstar.com.au/life-insurance/income-protection-insurance/.

XVII.  Canstar https://www.canstar.com.au/life-insurance/trauma-insurance/

XVIII.  Australian Institute of Health and Welfare. Australian Government. https://www.aihw.gov.au/reports/older-people/older-australia-at-a-glance/contents/demographics-of-older-australian

www.ingramcontent.com/pod-product-compliance
Lightning Source LLC
Chambersburg PA
CBHW071425210326
41597CB00020B/3653